What Shall We Name the Baby?

by **Warren W. Wiersbe**
General Director
Back to the Bible

Back to the Bible

Lincoln, Nebraska 68501

55,000 printed to date—1987
(5-5240—55M—47)
ISBN 0-8474-6516-0

Cover illustration and design by Robert Greuter & Associates

Printed in the United States of America

Contents

Chapter   **Page**

1. Man of Clay 5
   Adam

2. The Life-Giver 16
   Eve

3. A Murderer and a Martyr 26
   Cain and Abel

4. Baby "Laughter" 39
   Isaac

5. Father Names the Baby 51
   Benjamin

6. Remembering to Forget 62
   Ephraim and Manasseh

7. The Baby Who Rescued His People 74
   Moses

8. Help for a Stranger 86
   Gershom and Eliezer

9. Babies, the Gift of God 97
   Samuel

10. Babies, an Answer to Prayer 109
    John the Baptist

11. The Greatest Baby of All 121
    Jesus Christ

12. Your New Name 132

Contents

Chap.		Page

1. Introductory

2. A Modern Israel in Making

3. Two Thousand Years

4. Why the Jews?

5. Assimilation and Nationality

6. Zionism

7. The "National Home" Policy

8. Britain's Mandate

9. The Jew and the Arab

10. Partition

11. Civil War

12. British and Arab

13. Britain, the Great Gold Brick

14. America's Answer to Power

15. The Essential Basis of a Jewish State

16. From Theory to Actuality

Chapter 1

Man of Clay

Adam

What shall we name the baby? Sometimes choosing a name for a baby can be a problem. My wife and I have some friends who didn't know what to name their fifth child when he was born. In fact, they didn't decide on a name until just before they left the hospital with the baby.

If your baby is a boy, you could go back to the oldest name in human history—the name Adam. In a recent survey here in Nebraska, Adam ranked tenth among popular names for boys. But it's actually a name that all of us bear, for we all belong to Adam's family.

We want to look at some of the babies in the Bible and examine their names to see what spiritual lessons we can learn. Our first two chapters will not deal with babies because we want to look at Adam and Eve, who did not start life as babies. But we can learn several important lessons from their names.

We find the account of the creation of Adam and Eve in Genesis 1:26-28: "And God said, Let us make man in our image, after our likeness; and let them have dominion over the fish of the sea, and over the

5

fowl of the air, and over the cattle, and over all the earth, and over every creeping thing that creepeth upon the earth. So God created man in his own image, in the image of God created he him; male and female created he them. And God blessed them, and God said unto them, Be fruitful, and multiply, and fill the earth, and subdue it; and have dominion over the fish of the sea, and over the fowl of the air, and over every living thing that moveth upon the earth."

Genesis 2:7 adds this comment: "And the Lord God formed man of the dust of the ground, and breathed into his nostrils the breath of life; and man became a living soul." Genesis 5:1,2 gives us the name we want to examine: "This is the book of the generations of Adam. In the day that God created man, in the likeness of God made he him; male and female created he them; and blessed them, and called their name Adam, in the day when they were created."

The name Adam means "earth," possibly "ruddy, or red, earth." We find a related name in Genesis 25:30—Edom. Esau was given the nickname "Edom," or "red," after he sold his birthright for some red pottage. So the name Adam refers to the red earth from which man was made.

There are actually four different Hebrew words used predominantly for man throughout the Bible. One word means "the earth." Another means "the male as opposed to the female." A third word means "a warrior, a strong man." The fourth word means "the frail, weak man." The name Adam,

6

which means "earth," is important because it teaches us so much about ourselves. It's good to know your family background, and we have some very special reminders of our background, our roots, whenever we consider the name Adam.

Where We Came From

The name Adam reminds us, first of all, *where we came from.* God formed man from the dust of the ground. The Hebrew word translated "ground" comes from the word "Adam." As Genesis 2:7 reminds us, "The Lord God formed man [Adam] of the dust of the ground, and breathed into his nostrils the breath of life; and man became a living soul."

It's important for us to remember where we came from because this helps us understand how we are supposed to live and what we are supposed to do with our lives. I think one of the problems with young people today is that they are being taught that they came from animals. They reason that if they evolved from an animal, they might as well live like an animal. This is why we see lawlessness and immorality among young people—and adults— because people are acting worse than animals.

Created by God

Thinking of the name Adam reminds us that *we were created by God.* At least 20 texts in the Bible specifically state that we were created by God. We didn't evolve—we were created. The Lord Jesus Christ Himself talked about the creation of the man and the woman (Matt. 19:4). In fact, God is still involved in this matter of the creation of human life whenever a baby is conceived.

Psalm 139:13-16 says, "For thou hast possessed my reins: thou hast covered me in my mother's womb. I will praise thee; for I am fearfully and wonderfully made: marvellous are thy works; and that my soul knoweth right well. My substance was not hid from thee, when I was made in secret, and curiously wrought in the lowest parts of the earth. Thine eyes did see my substance, yet being unperfect; and in thy book all my members were written." In other words, this passage states that the conception and formation of a baby is still supervised by God.

This does not mean that God is responsible for what may happen to a baby because his mother or father didn't behave. It's unfortunate when a baby is born handicapped in some way because of the disobedience and sin of the parents. What the psalmist was emphasizing here is that God knows about the conception of every baby. He is there to supervise; and if there is some problem, God knows all about it and will work it out for His glory. God is still, in this sense, creating people.

Created in God's Image

We were created by God, and we were also *created in God's image.* "So God created man in his own image, in the image of God created he him; male and female created he them" (Gen. 1:27). This means that we have personality. We have a mind to

8

think with, emotions to feel with and a will to decide with. We also have a spiritual aspect to our nature. Did you notice in Genesis 2:7 that man is a combination of dust and deity? God formed man from the dust and then breathed life into him. We are a combination of earth and heaven. We have a fleshly nature that defeats us and brings us down, and yet we have a spirit within us that wants to reach up to God. The unsaved person has a dead spirit within, but that spirit can be made alive through faith in Jesus Christ.

When you tell children that they are made in the image of God, they begin to sense the dignity of being human. But if you tell them that they evolved from animals, then they will act like animals! Because we were created in the image of God, we are responsible to our Creator. We need to live responsibly, respecting the image of God in our fellowman. All that we possess has been given to us from God. Remembering that we are created in God's image helps us realize what God has really done for us.

Created From the Dust

The name Adam reminds us where we came from: We were created by God and created in His image. But we were also *created from the dust.* "And the Lord God formed man of the dust of the ground" (Gen. 2:7). This means that man is composed of the basic elements of the earth. Man is weak because he is made from dust. Sometimes we think we are made from steel, but we are really made from dust. We often forget that we are made from dust and begin to act as if we're going to live forever. God, however, remembers our composition and knows our weaknesses: "Like as a father pitieth his children, so the Lord pitieth them that fear him. For he knoweth our frame; he remembereth that we are dust" (Ps. 103:13,14).

Regarding the weakness of our flesh, we find an interesting phrase in Job 4:19: "How much less in them that dwell in houses of clay, whose foundation is in the dust, which are crushed before the moth?" In the context we find that Eliphaz was asking Job a question. In verse 18 he reminded Job that God "put no trust in his servants; and his angels he charged with folly." So Eliphaz was asking, "How much less then is God going to pay attention to men and women, who dwell in houses of clay?" To live in a house of clay whose foundation is on stones would be all right, but to live in a house of clay that has its foundation in the dust is very perilous. In fact, Eliphaz said it could be destroyed even by a moth!

Our physical body is like living in a house of clay made from the dust. That is a good illustration of our weakness. But there is great potential in that dust. Another picture we need to see is that of the potter and the clay. The Hebrew word "formed" used in Genesis 2:7 is a potter's term and is translated "potter" in Jeremiah 18:4: "And the vessel that he made of clay was marred in the hand of the potter: so he made it again." God made us out of clay because clay has tremendous potential.

God wants to make something out of our lives.

Why did He create us to begin with? Isaiah 43:7 says, "I have created him for my glory, I have formed him; yea, I have made him." That's pretty explicit. God made us for His glory. Our house of clay has marvelous potential. God can mold us and shape us according to His will. That's why we shouldn't resist Him. We should allow Him to do what He chooses with us. "Woe unto him that striveth with his Maker! Let the potsherd strive with the potsherds of the earth. Shall the clay say to him that fashioneth it, What makest thou? or thy work, He hath no hands?" (45:9). This verse points out how foolish it would be for the clay to question or fight with the potter. The clay yields to the potter and lets him have his way. And as Isaiah 64:8 reminds us, "But now, O Lord, thou art our father; we are the clay, and thou our potter; and we all are the work of thy hand."

Because we are all made from one material—dust—there's a oneness to mankind. "He giveth to all life, and breath, and all things; and hath made of one blood all nations of men" (Acts 17:25,26). Remembering this should help us to be patient and understanding of others. It should humble us to remember we came from dust.

Where We Are Going

When we think of the name Adam, it should not only remind us where we came from but also *where we are going*. We came from the dust, and we will return to the dust. Adam and Eve wanted to be like

11

God (see Gen. 3:5), but they ended up being dust! After Adam and Eve sinned, God said to Adam, "Because thou hast hearkened unto the voice of thy wife, and hast eaten of the tree, of which I commanded thee, saying, Thou shalt not eat of it: cursed is the ground for thy sake; in sorrow shalt thou eat of it all the days of thy life; thorns also and thistles shall it bring forth to thee; and thou shalt eat the herb of the field; in the sweat of thy face shalt thou eat bread, till thou return unto the ground; for out of it wast thou taken: for dust thou art, and unto dust shalt thou return" (vv. 17-19).

Adam's sin brought death to the entire human race. Romans 5:12 says, "Wherefore, as by one man sin entered into the world, and death by sin; and so death passed upon all men, for that all have sinned." Where did we come from? The dust. Where are we going? To the dust. Adam, as the head of the old creation, plunged everything into the dust of death. That's why the Lord Jesus Christ had to come. "For since by man [Adam] came death, by man [Christ] came also the resurrection of the dead. For as in Adam all die, even so in Christ shall all be made alive" (I Cor. 15:21,22).

Our bodies are going to return to dust someday if we die before the Lord returns, but there's going to be a resurrection. The Lord Jesus will return and raise the dead; then we will have new bodies. But until then we must face death. "For out of it [the ground] wast thou taken: for dust thou art, and unto dust shalt thou return" (Gen. 3:19). Every baby born into the world has to immediately start

12

struggling against death, because we're going back to the dust.

We know where we are eventually going, but the question is, Are you prepared? Are you afraid to face death and judgment? If you are, then you'll be glad to know what God has done for you. "For the wages of sin is death; but the gift of God is eternal life through Jesus Christ our Lord" (Rom. 6:23).

What We Must Do

The name Adam not only reminds us where we came from (the dust) and where we're going (the dust), but it also tells us *what we must do*. Because the first Adam plunged us into the dust of death, God sent another Adam to redeem us. We know this from I Corinthians 15:42-49. "The first man Adam was made a living soul; the last Adam [Jesus Christ] was made a quickening [life-giving] spirit" (v. 45).

In this passage, the Apostle Paul contrasted the first Adam with the last Adam. The first Adam was the head of the old creation. Jesus, the last Adam, is the head of a new creation. Adam failed in a garden (Eden) and disobeyed God, but the Lord Jesus Christ yielded in a garden (Gethsemane) and obeyed God. He said, "Not my will, but thine, be done" (Luke 22:42). Adam said, "My will." Jesus Christ said, "Thy will." The first Adam brought sin and death into this world, but the last Adam brought righteousness and life into the world. The first Adam was a thief; he was caught stealing from a tree and was cast out of Paradise. The last Adam

13

turned to a thief and said, "To day shalt thou be with me in paradise" (Luke 23:43). The first Adam hid behind a tree, trying to run from God. The last Adam was hanged on a tree, bearing your sins and mine.

The first Adam brought us into difficulty, destruction, death and dust. The last Adam brings us victory and life—eternal life and eternal glory. God wants to restore His image in you and me, and it begins with salvation. "But if our gospel be hid, it is hid to them that are lost: in whom the god of this world hath blinded the minds of them which believe not, lest the light of the glorious gospel of Christ, who is the image of God, should shine unto them. . . . For God, who commanded the light to shine out of darkness, hath shined in our hearts, to give the light of the knowledge of the glory of God in the face of Jesus Christ" (II Cor. 4:3,4,6).

The restoration of God's image begins when we let the light of Jesus Christ shine in our hearts. It begins with salvation; it continues with sanctification. As we walk with the Lord, the image of God is renewed in our lives. "Lie not one to another, seeing that ye have put off the old man with his deeds; and have put on the new man, which is [being] renewed in knowledge after the image of him that created him" (Col. 3:9,10). That's the Christian life—being recreated in God's image. And though our bodies may one day end in dust (if we die before the Lord's return), our spirit will go home to be with the Lord.

The last step to restoring God's image will be glorification—when we shall be like the Lord Jesus

14

Christ. Romans 8:29 says, "For whom he did foreknow, he also did predestinate to be conformed to the image of his Son." But the Lord Jesus had to go down into the dust of death to make everlasting life possible for us (Ps. 22:15). He was made a curse; He bore all the sorrows, all the pain, all the thorns for us because of Adam's sin.

Genesis 5:1 begins, "This is the book of the generations of Adam." Matthew 1:1 begins, "The book of the generation of Jesus Christ." How we ought to thank God that He sent Jesus Christ to be the last Adam! Death no longer holds terror for us because we can look forward to going to heaven.

The name Adam reminds us where we came from. We were created by God, in His image, from the dust of the ground; but that dust has tremendous potential. "Adam" also reminds us where we are going—back to the dust. By his sin, Adam plunged all of creation into the dust of death. But the name Adam also reminds us that there is a second, and a last, Adam—Jesus Christ. Because of His death on our behalf, we know what we must do. We must trust Him for our salvation. In order to restore the image of God that Adam's sin effaced, we must place our faith in Christ for salvation, sanctification and glorification. Do you belong to Jesus Christ, the last Adam? Have you trusted Him?

Chapter 2

The Life-Giver

Eve

What shall we name the baby? If it's a girl, we could name her Eve. That was the first name given to a woman, and it was given to the first woman. The Hebrew word for Eve means "living" or "life-giver." We find in Genesis 3:20 that Adam named his wife Eve: "And Adam called his wife's name Eve; because she was the mother of all living." You will remember that at creation she was called "Adam": "Male and female created he them; and blessed them, and called their name Adam, in the day when they were created" (5:2). Even though Eve was made from the side of Adam, she was still given the name Adam because that side came from the ground. All of us, male and female, are made of dust and return to the dust when we die. And so the woman was called "Adam," because she would one day return to the earth just as her husband would.

It's important to notice that the woman was created by the same God who created man and that she was created in the same image. "And God said, Let us make man in our image, after our likeness: and let them have dominion over the fish of the sea, and over the fowl of the air, and over the cattle, and over all the earth, and over every creeping thing that creepeth upon the earth. So God created man in his own image, in the image of God created he him; male and female created he them. And God blessed them, and God said unto them, Be fruitful, and multiply, and replenish [fill] the earth, and subdue it: and have dominion" (Gen. 1:26-28). Even though Eve was made later, she shared the image of God with Adam. She was created by the same marvelous Creator. And she shared in ruling the earth: "God blessed them, and [gave them] dominion" (v. 28). Eve shared in the same blessing; therefore, she was the queen of the old creation just as Adam was the king of the old creation. I think it was Matthew Henry who wrote that if God made man the head, He made woman the crown. And that is a wonderful description.

When God first brought Adam his bride in the Garden, Adam said, "This is now bone of my bones, and flesh of my flesh: she shall be called Woman, because she was taken out of Man" (2:23). God had called the first woman "Adam," and He gave her equality with Adam in creation, in His image and in His blessing. Adam called her "Woman," and then one day he named her "Eve."

A Declaration of Adam's Faith

We need to consider the significance of this name. When Adam called his wife's name "Eve," it was, first of all, *a declaration of his faith.* "And Adam called his wife's name Eve; because she was

17

the mother of all living" (Gen. 3:20). When did he do this? It was after God had pronounced judgment on the serpent, on the woman, on the man and on the ground.

Genesis 3 is the story of man's fall. The serpent tempted Eve, and she tempted Adam. Because of Adam's sin, death and judgment came upon all creation. In Adam all men die. When Adam and Eve sinned, they tried to run away and hide from God and to cover their sin. But God found them. I can't prove it, but I believe that when God called out to Adam, "Where art thou?" (v. 9), it was not with the stern voice of a police officer looking for a criminal. I believe it was with the brokenhearted tones of a loving father whose heart was heavy because his children had rebelled against him.

The setting is one of sin and judgment, but we still see the loving heart of a Heavenly Father at work. It's interesting to notice that God cursed the serpent and the ground out of which man came, but He did not curse the woman or the man. "God said unto the serpent, Because thou hast done this, thou art cursed above all cattle, and above every beast of the field; upon thy belly shalt thou go, and dust shalt thou eat all the days of thy life" (v. 14).

Then we read that great statement that theologians call the first giving of the Gospel: "And I will put enmity between thee and the woman, and between thy seed and her seed; [he] shall bruise thy head, and thou shalt bruise his heel" (v. 15). In this verse God declared war on Satan by saying, in effect, "You and mankind will experience conflict

18

and strife throughout history, but ultimately the seed of the woman will be victorious."

God declared war on Satan but not on man. The woman was not cursed; however, her sorrow was multiplied as a consequence of her sin (v. 16). I do not think that God put a judgment on Eve as though motherhood and the bearing of children were some kind of a curse. No, He simply said to her, "Because sin has now come into your life, that which could have been much more beautiful and much more wonderful—the bearing of children—is going to have pain and sorrow attached to it" (see v. 16). God was saying to the woman, "Just as the man is going to have to deal with problems as he tills the earth and seeks to earn his daily bread, so you are going to have burdens to bear and battles to fight as you fulfill your purposes in this world."

In the midst of this sorrowful news, God gave Adam and Eve hope for the future. Genesis 3:15 is God's promise that one day a Redeemer would come. When God announced that conflict and hatred would exist between the children of the woman and the children of the Devil, He also promised ultimate victory for man. "I will put enmity between thee and the woman, and between thy seed [children, descendants] and her seed" (v. 15).

It's interesting to see from this verse that the Devil has a family. Who are the Devil's children? The Lord Jesus once said to the Pharisees, "You are of your father, the Devil. He is a murderer and a liar" (see John 8:44). The first child of the Devil in human history was Cain. He was a liar and a murderer, for he killed his brother and then lied about it (Gen. 4:8,9). Satan's family is a self-righteous, religious family. But their righteousness doesn't come from heaven; it comes from hell. They may even appear to have a religious morality, but it is not truly the righteousness of Jesus Christ. One member of Satan's family stands out as his ultimate production— the Antichrist. This world ruler born of Satan is going to be Satan's great masterpiece. History will culminate in the great battle between Christ and Antichrist (II Thess. 2).

Who is the woman's seed in Genesis 3:15? Ultimately, it is referring to the Lord Jesus Christ. God used a woman to bring the Saviour into the world. We find God's first promise in this verse: "I will put enmity." Throughout Scripture you'll find many promises—"I will" statements—made by God. But this is the greatest of them all: "I will one day send the seed of the woman, and He will crush Satan's head, although Satan will bruise His heel."

Now we can begin to see the significance of why Adam named his wife "Eve." He believed God's promise recorded in Genesis 3:15. That's how Adam and Eve were saved. By faith they believed God's word. Salvation has always been by faith.

Genesis 5:1 says, "This is the book of the generations of Adam." You could apply that statement to the entire Old Testament, for it records the details of the children of Adam. And every one of Adam's children failed in one way or another. When you turn to Matthew 1:1, you read: "The book of the generation of Jesus Christ." God began to write a new book with the New Testament, and He started a new family. "For as in Adam all die, even so in Christ shall all be made alive" (I Cor. 15:22). How does the Old Testament end? "Lest I come and smite the earth with a curse" (Mal. 4:6). What does the New Testament declare? "And there shall be no more curse" (Rev. 22:3). Whose family are you in—Adam's or Christ's? Adam believed God, and naming his wife Eve was an evidence and declaration of his faith.

A Description of Eve's Ministry

Eve's name (life-giver) is not only a declaration of Adam's faith; it is also *a description of Eve's ministry.* Death came through Adam, but life came through Eve. I can say this because it was through the bearing of a child that redemption came into the world. When Mary gave birth to the Lord Jesus Christ, she was fulfilling Genesis 3:15. Because Jesus came into this world, we can have eternal life.

Certainly Eve was a life-giver in a physical sense. I think the Lord was talking in this passage about the ministry of motherhood. And it is a ministry! We must not criticize those who have *not* entered into this ministry, for God has different callings and gifts for different people. But motherhood is a ministry to which He calls woman. Psalm 113:9 says, "He maketh the barren woman to keep house, and to be a joyful mother of children. Praise ye the Lord." I hope that every mother is joyful and, in spite of the burdens and the pain, can say, "Praise ye the Lord."

21

Psalm 127 reminds us what a blessing children are: "Lo, children are an heritage of the Lord: and the fruit of the womb is his reward. As arrows are in the hand of a mighty man; so are children of the youth. Happy is the man that hath his quiver full of them: they shall not be ashamed, but they shall speak with the enemies in the gate" (vv. 3-5).

Did you know that God describes Himself not only as a father but also as a spiritual mother? Isaiah 49:15 says, "Can a woman forget her sucking child, that she should not have compassion on the son of her womb? yea, they may forget, yet will I not forget thee." God is comparing Himself here to a mother who would give herself for her child. We read in Isaiah 66:13: "As one whom his mother comforteth, so will I comfort you; and ye shall be comforted in Jerusalem." God ministers to us like a mother as well as like a father.

The ministry of motherhood is a godly ministry. I'm sure many of us can give thanks for mothers who prayed for us, taught us and saw to it that we were in Sunday school and church.

We find an interesting verse in I Timothy 2:15 that talks about bearing children: "Notwithstanding she shall be saved in childbearing, if they continue in faith and charity and holiness with sobriety." Some have understood this verse to mean that if a Christian couple is walking with the Lord, God will give the wife salvation in childbirth—not eternal life but physical safety. In other words, God will take her through motherhood, or through the birth of the child, successfully. After all, when a woman gives birth to a child, she descends into the valley of the shadow of death.

But I think there's another possible interpretation of I Timothy 2:15, because the Greek says, "She shall be saved in *the* childbearing." I wonder if Paul wasn't referring to the bearing of the great Child, the Lord Jesus Christ. After all, how are men and women saved? Through the Lord Jesus Christ. No one inherits salvation. "But as many as received him, to them gave he power to become the sons of God, even to them that believe on his name: which were born, not of blood [not by inheritance from your parents], nor of the will of the flesh [not by self-effort], nor of the will of man [not by the efforts of others], but of God" (John 1:12,13). Salvation comes through trusting Jesus Christ by faith alone. There is no other way of salvation.

A Demonstration of God's Grace

The name Eve is a declaration of Adam's faith. He believed God's word, and God saved him. It is also the description of Eve's ministry—the ministry of motherhood. Women down through the ages in the Old Testament were looking for the birth of the Messiah, and at last the Messiah came. Finally, the name Eve is *a demonstration of God's grace.* Genesis 3:20 says, "And Adam called his wife's name Eve; because she was the mother of all living." How did God respond to this? Verse 21 says, "Unto Adam also and to his wife did the Lord God make coats of skins, and clothed them."

God responded to their faith, saved them and

23

forgave them; and He symbolized that by clothing them. God wants us to be covered, not only physically but spiritually. You can always tell when a nation is starting to decline morally because it begins to take off its clothes. In the Bible nudity is termed a sin. So God clothed Adam and Eve physically, but it was a picture of their spiritual covering. The covering that they had made, aprons of leaves, was not acceptable to God. He said, "No, you cannot be covered by your own works. I have to cover you." And when He covered them, it wasn't with leaves; He covered them with skins. This meant that some animals had to die. So from the very beginning we have the concept that blood must be shed for our sins to be covered. God can forgive and accept us on the basis of the shed blood.

This raises an interesting question: What is your covering today? Are you trusting a covering, for example, of good works? Will they be sufficient to cover you? Consider Isaiah 64:6: "We are all as an unclean thing, and all our righteousnesses are as filthy rags." If God considers all of our righteous deeds to be filthy rags, how must He look at our sins? No, God won't accept our robe of self-righteousness as a covering. He wants us to be clothed in that wonderful robe of righteousness that only He can give. "I will greatly rejoice in the Lord, my soul shall be joyful in my God; for he hath clothed me with the garments of salvation, he hath covered me with the robe of righteousness, as a bridegroom decketh himself with ornaments, and as a bride adorneth herself with her jewels" (61:10).

God wraps us in the righteousness of Jesus Christ, and we don't have to put on our filthy rags of self-righteousness. Another illustration of this is found in the story of the Prodigal Son. When the Prodigal Son came home, his father said, "Bring forth the best robe, and put it on him" (Luke 15:22).

When God clothed Adam and Eve in the garments made from animal skins, it was a demonstration of His grace. Adam had believed God's promise and named his wife Eve. In response, God clothed Adam and Eve in the righteousness of His Son. As you read further in the Bible, you see this marvelous truth revealed: "For he hath made him to be sin for us, who knew no sin; that we might be made the righteousness of God in him" (II Cor. 5:21).

Adam called his wife Eve (life-giver). It was a declaration of his faith. Have you declared your faith? Have you believed God's Word, or are you still listening to the Devil's lies? It was a description of Eve's ministry of motherhood—bringing life into the world and giving us eternal life through Jesus Christ. And it was a demonstration of God's grace. He responded to that name. He clothed them, and in order to do that, there had to be a sacrifice. Have you been clothed in the righteousness of Jesus Christ? Nothing else will do.

Chapter 3

A Murderer and a Martyr

Cain and Abel

Have you ever known a family in which you would never guess that the children belong to the same parents? Maybe the children look nothing alike. Or perhaps their personalities are completely different. I'm sure that most of us know some Christian parents who are struggling with a "black sheep" in their family. Even though the child was raised to know the Lord, he has chosen to rebel against his parents' instruction. Parents in this situation may ask themselves, *Why am I having so much trouble with this child when the others are so good? What have I done wrong?*

Adam and Eve may have asked themselves these same questions. Their sons, the first two babies born in the world, were nothing alike. Even though Cain and Abel were brothers, even though they had been raised in the same family with the same upbringing and influence, their lives turned out so differently. Why? Because their hearts were different. While environment and parental guidance are important, in the end what really counts is the person's attitudes and motives.

The names given to the first two children of the Bible reveal much about their lives—and about ours. Genesis 4:1,2 tells us, "And Adam knew Eve his wife; and she conceived, and bare Cain, and said, I have gotten a man from the Lord. And she again bare his brother Abel. And Abel was a keeper of sheep, but Cain was a tiller of the ground."

As Eve held her firstborn son in her arms, she may have reflected back on God's promise that the seed of the woman would crush the head of the serpent (see 3:15). She named the baby "Cain," which means "acquired, gotten." Possibly Eve believed that this baby boy was the promised redeemer. Another way to translate Genesis 4:1 is "I have gotten a man, even the Lord." While Eve could have believed that Cain was the Lord's chosen one, I think she was simply acknowledging the fact that her child came from God.

Throughout the Bible we are told that children are a gift from God. In Psalm 127:3 we read: "Lo, children are an heritage of the Lord: and the fruit of the womb is his reward." Children are given to us as a blessing and reward. Unfortunately, too many parents view their children as a burden—an intrusion that prevents them from doing everything they want to. As we have seen, this kind of attitude leads to trouble in the family. Like Eve, we need to regard our children as a gift from the Lord—a blessing to be enjoyed, nurtured and protected.

Soon after the birth of Cain, Eve conceived again and gave birth to another son. She named her second child "Abel," a name meaning "vanity,

27

breath." It is the same Hebrew word that is used in the Book of Ecclesiastes some 37 times: "Vanity of vanities; all is vanity" (1:2). We don't know what prompted Eve to give her baby this name. She may have begun to see the reality of her sin and its result—death. She may have realized just how fleeting life is. Eve had no idea how prophetic her choice of names would be. Because Cain did not acquire the same blessing given to Abel by God, he killed his brother in a fit of jealousy. In an instant Abel's life was gone like a vapor, a breath.

The life, and name, of Abel reminds us that our time on earth is not as permanent as we may think. The writer James reflected this truth when he stated, "Go to now, ye that say, To day or to morrow we will go into such a city, and continue there a year, and buy and sell, and get gain: whereas ye know not what shall be on the morrow. For what is your life? It is even a vapour, that appeareth for a little time, and then vanisheth away. For that ye ought to say, If the Lord will, we shall live, and do this, or that. But now ye rejoice in your boastings: all such rejoicing is evil. Therefore to him that knoweth to do good, and doeth it not, to him it is sin" (James 4:13-17).

In this passage, James warned us not to become arrogant about our lives. We make plans, leaving the Lord out of them entirely. We decide that we are going to take a certain job in a certain city for a certain length of time and make a certain amount of money. But we have no guarantee that we will still be on earth tomorrow. Life is a vapor that has a way of vanishing before we know it. Rather than boasting about *our* big plans, we should seek the Lord's will in everything, remembering that each day of life is a gift from Him.

The names of Cain and Abel represent two different aspects of life. Man is a combination of dust and destiny, of heaven and earth. God made us out of the dust of the ground and then breathed into us the breath of life. Thus, we are a mixture of the temporary and the eternal. At death the body returns to the dust from which it came, while the spirit enters eternity. We need to continually remember that the Lord gives us life. But our life on earth is only temporary—a mere breath. Soon the Lord will take us out of the world again. That's why it's important to know Jesus Christ as your Saviour. When you belong to Christ, then your life is not just a breath. You have not lived in vain, for "he that doeth the will of God abideth for ever" (I John 2:17).

Cain and Abel were as different as their names. It is hard for us to understand why they turned out so differently when they had so much in common. They had the same heredity—they were both the sons of Adam and Eve. They were raised in the same environment and had the same example set for them. They had the same devotion to duty; Abel watched the sheep, while Cain worked in the fields. These brothers were not lazy. They worked hard instead of looking for ways to escape responsibility. They also would have received the same training. Their parents knew God and surely taught the boys how to worship the Lord and walk with Him. It is

29

evident from the Scriptures that these young men were religious. In Genesis 4:3-5 we find them coming to present their offerings at the altar: "And in process of time it came to pass, that Cain brought of the fruit of the ground an offering unto the Lord. And Abel, he also brought of the firstlings of his flock and of the fat thereof. And the Lord had respect unto Abel and to his offering: but unto Cain and to his offering he had not respect."

Cain and Abel had a great deal in common. They both worked hard and then brought offerings to God from their labors. So why did the Lord accept Abel and his offering while rejecting Cain and his sacrifice? Because while these men appeared to be the same on the outside, their hearts were different. They had different motives and attitudes as they presented their offerings to God. It is this contrast that explains why Cain became a murderer while Abel became a martyr.

A Contrast in Worship

As we examine the lives of Cain and Abel, we notice three areas of contrast between these two brothers. First, we see *a contrast in their worship.* At first glance, this contrast is not apparent. Cain and Abel both believed in God; Cain was not an atheist or an agnostic. It appears that they received the same instruction and example from their parents. They came to the same altar at the same time. So how was their worship different? Abel presented the offering God had prescribed; Cain did not.

Because Cain refused to worship God in the manner He had ordained, his offering was not acceptable to the Lord.

What were God's instructions concerning worship? I believe that when God clothed Adam and Eve in the Garden, He set the example for how He wanted them to worship. Genesis 3:21 states, "Unto Adam also and to his wife did the Lord God make coats of skins, and clothed them." In order for the Lord to make these coats of skins, He had to kill an innocent animal. Thus, animal sacrifices became the pattern of worship throughout the Old Testament age. The only way to cover the sins of the people, from Adam and Eve onward, was through the shedding of blood. From the beginning, God established a pattern of worship that pointed the way to Christ, who became the final and complete sacrifice for man's sins.

In the light of God's instructions to Adam and Eve, the difference in the offerings of Cain and Abel becomes apparent. Abel came to the altar by faith; Cain did not. We find this confirmed in Hebrews 11:4: "By faith Abel offered unto God a more excellent sacrifice than Cain, by which he obtained witness that he was righteous, God testifying of his gifts: and by it he being dead yet speaketh."

The contrast we see in the worship of Cain and Abel is the difference between faith and unbelief. Roman 10:17 says, "Faith cometh by hearing, and hearing by the word of God." Abel was exercising faith in the Word of God. Abel knew God's instructions for sacrifice, and he brought the right offering—a sacrifice of blood. He also offered it with the right attitude; his heart was in the right place. He brought the very best of his flock. Therefore, God accepted Abel's worship: "And the Lord had respect unto Abel and to his offering" (Gen. 4:4).

Cain, on the other hand, had religion without faith. He was merely going through the motions of worship. He was concerned only with the external—he wanted to look religious to others. His heart was not right with God. Many "Christians" today are guilty of the same surface religion. They are like the false teachers described by Jude. These false teachers were said to be following the "way of Cain" (Jude 1:11).

The Scriptures tell us that God bore witness to Abel and to his sacrifice (see Heb. 11:4). How did Abel know that God had honored his sacrifice? I believe the Lord placed this conviction in his heart. He gave him the confidence and peace that enabled him to know he was right with God through faith. In addition, while the text does not indicate that God confirmed Abel's offering with a sign, it is possible that He sent fire from heaven to consume the sacrifice. So Abel probably received both an inward and an outward witness that he belonged to God.

But Cain received no such witness. God did not respect Cain because his heart was full of unbelief. Likewise, the Lord did not accept Cain's sacrifice because it was not the kind of offering He wanted. When Cain learned that God had rejected his offering, he "was very wroth [angry], and his countenance fell" (Gen. 4:5). I can just see him standing by the altar pouting. He was angry at God and at his brother when, in reality, he should have been angry at himself for doing something so foolish.

"And the Lord said unto Cain, Why art thou [angry]? and why is thy countenance fallen? If thou doest well, shalt not be accepted?" (vv. 6,7). As Cain stood by the altar fuming, the Lord told him, in effect, "Why are you angry with Me. You know what I have told you; believe it and act on it. When you do, then I will accept you and your sacrifice just as I have honored your brother and his worship."

The Lord knew the anger and jealousy brewing in Cain's heart, and with His explanation He issued a warning: "If thou doest not well, sin lieth at the door. And unto thee shall be his desire, and thou shalt rule over him" (v. 7). The Hebrew word translated "lieth" in this verse portrays the image of a lion crouching at the door. Thus, God was telling Cain, in essence, "Be careful when you leave, because temptation is waiting to pounce on you."

Because Cain was not worshiping the Lord as he should, he lost his authority and power. Life became too much for him. His unbelief had weakened his spirit to the point where he was easy prey for Satan. A lack of true worship is the first step on the path to sin. When our relationship with God is wrong, it becomes impossible for us to respond in the right way to the people and circumstances in God's world. For this reason, it is vital that we have faith in God through the Lord Jesus Christ.

33

A Contrast in Works

The worship of Cain and Abel reveals the difference between faith and unbelief. Because their motives for worship were different, there was also *a contrast in their works*.

What was the difference between the works of Cain and the works of Abel? We find the answer in I John 3: "In this the children of God are manifest, and the children of the devil: whosoever doeth not righteousness is not of God, neither he that loveth not his brother. For this is the message that ye heard from the beginning, that we should love one another. Not as Cain, who was of that wicked one, and slew his brother. And wherefore slew he him? Because his own works were evil, and his brother's righteous. . . . We know that we have passed from death unto life, because we love the brethren. He that loveth not his brother abideth in death" (vv. 10-12,14).

Abel's works stand in contrast to those of Cain because his were righteous in God's eyes while Cain's were evil. God considered Abel's works to be righteous for two reasons. First, they were the result of faith. When you have faith in God, you naturally have the desire to do His work. If you don't, then you do not have true faith, for faith without works is dead (James 2:20). The second reason Abel's works were righteous is because they glorified the Lord. His motive for worship was to praise and honor God. He did not want to draw attention to himself and his "righteousness."

Even though Cain was at the altar, making a sacrifice to God, the Bible tells us that his works were evil. Why? Because Satan was in charge (see I John 3:12). What were Cain's works? His first work was unbelief. He rejected God's word and therefore, in essence, called the Lord a liar. Second, he was guilty of the works of envy and hatred. When you have "an evil heart of unbelief" (Heb. 3:12), you commit sin after sin. Cain's unbelief caused him to envy his brother. Then he began to hate Abel. This hatred eventually led him to murder his brother: "And Cain talked with Abel his brother: and it came to pass, when they were in the field, that Cain rose up against Abel his brother, and slew him. And the Lord said unto Cain, Where is Abel thy brother? And he said, I know not: Am I my brother's keeper? And he said, What hast thou done? the voice of thy brother's blood crieth unto me from the ground. And now art thou cursed from the earth, which hath opened her mouth to receive thy brother's blood from thy hand" (Gen. 4:8-11).

Cain killed his brother and then tried to lie about it to God. Because Cain was a child of the Devil, he was exhibiting the works of Satan. He was spiritually dead. Jesus warned us about what happens when we allow Satan to control us: "Ye are of your father the devil, and the lusts of your father ye will do. He was a murderer from the beginning, and abode not in the truth, because there is no truth in him. When he speaketh a lie, he speaketh of his own: for he is a liar, and the father of it" (John 8:44). In this passage, Jesus wasn't talking to irreligious sinners. He was speaking to the religious and self-righteous Pharisees.

Like the Pharisees, Cain (the "acquired" one) thought he could earn God's approval by his works. He discovered too late that God's basis for acceptance is *faith*. Works are merely an outgrowth of our faith and worship. Thus, Cain's works were evil because his worship was wrong. The god you worship will determine the works you practice.

A Contrast in Witness

The third thing we see in the lives of Cain and Abel is *a contrast in their witness*. Cain was a liar and a murderer; therefore, he had no witness for the truth. After he sinned, he was concerned only about punishment, not confession. When God confronted Cain with his sin and pronounced judgment on him, Cain lamented, "My punishment is greater than I can bear" (Gen. 4:13). Notice that Cain didn't say, "My sin and guilt are greater than I can bear."

Cain is a picture of the self-righteous, religious person who doesn't want God's way of salvation. This person is concerned only about punishment, not purity. He doesn't care about having a right relationship with God; he just wants to feel good. Those who choose to reject God will suffer the same fate as Cain, who became a fugitive and a wanderer (see vv. 12,14). The Hebrew word for "vagabond," or wanderer, means "to wander aimlessly." It depicts a person who is unstable and staggering around like a drunk in the street. He is like a reed in the water; he has no direction and purpose. Life without God lacks meaning and purpose. When a person tries to succeed by his own righteousness, he is destined to fail again and again.

Cain's "righteousness" made him a murderer and a fugitive. Abel, on the other hand, became a martyr for his faith. His primary concern was doing the Lord's will, and as a result, he received the respect and approval of God. Because of his relationship to God, Abel's witness is still heard today: "By faith Abel offered unto God a more excellent sacrifice than Cain, by which he obtained witness that he was righteous, God testifying of his gifts: and by it he being dead yet speaketh" (Heb. 11:4).

The life of Cain speaks to the wanderers, liars, murderers and unbelievers of this world about the results of rejecting God. In fact, his life parallels the description of the people who will spend eternity in hell (see Rev. 22:15). He is a witness of the evil that accompanies an attitude of self-righteousness and unbelief.

By contrast, the life of Abel is a witness of the great truth that you can be approved by God through faith. His blood still points the way to the Lord. But while Abel's death was significant, only Christ's sacrifice has eternal value. The blood of Abel cried out for judgment, but the blood of the Lord Jesus gives mercy and grace. Because of Abel's blood, Cain was driven away to become a wanderer. However, our Lord's blood opens the way for us to come home and become the children of God. Abel's blood speaks of death, but our Lord's blood speaks of eternal life.

Whose witness have you believed? Are you following the way of Cain—the way of unbelief, false worship and evil works? Or are you listening to the witness of Abel—the witness of the blood? In Cain we see the tragedy of unbelief—doing things our way. In Abel we see the blessing of faith—following God's way. Cain was a child of the Devil; Abel was a child of God. What made the difference? Their attitude toward God. The most important thing you and I can do today is to be sure our hearts are right with God by believing in the Lord Jesus Christ and having the right attitudes and motives for worship and service. What will you be—a murderer or a martyr for the truth?

Chapter 4

Baby "Laughter"

Isaac

How often do you laugh? Many Christians today have the mistaken idea that believers must be solemn all of the time. Thus, they miss much of the joy of the Christian life. The Bible tells us, "A merry heart doeth good like a medicine" (Prov. 17:22). Hearty laughter is not only therapeutic for the mind and the body, it is also good for the soul.

As you study the Bible, you will discover many heroes of the faith who laughed. They laughed for many reasons—out of joy, faith and even unbelief. In fact, the Lord even gave one important baby of the Bible a name that means "he laughs."

What is the name that means "he laughs"? We find the answer in Genesis 17: "And God said unto Abraham, As for Sarai thy wife, thou shalt not call her name Sarai, but Sarah shall her name be. And I will bless her, and give thee a son also of her: yea, I will bless her, and she shall be a mother of nations; kings of people shall be of her. Then Abraham fell upon his face, and laughed, and said in his heart, Shall a child be born unto him that is an hundred years old? and shall Sarah, that is ninety years old, bear? And Abraham said unto God, O that Ishmael might live before thee! And God said, Sarah thy wife shall bear thee a son indeed; and thou shalt call his name Isaac: and I will establish my covenant with him for an everlasting covenant, and with his seed after him" (vv. 15-19).

In this passage, the Lord spoke to Abraham and reaffirmed His promise to make Abraham a great nation (see 13:16). Abraham and Sarah had waited many years for the fulfillment of this promise, and yet they still did not have even one child, let alone a vast multitude of descendants. They were old and well past childbearing age. When Abraham heard that they were to have a child, he laughed. Because he laughed, God told him that the son they would bear should be named Isaac, a name meaning "he laughs."

God was about to perform one of the greatest miracles in history—a miracle that would not only bring joy to the lives of Abraham and Sarah but also would give birth to an entire nation. For this reason, Isaac was not the only one who received a name. His parents were given new names to remind them, and us, of what the Lord could do.

But before the Lord renamed Abram and Sarai, He gave Himself a new name: "I am the Almighty God; walk before me, and be thou perfect" (17:1). The Hebrew word translated "Almighty God" is *El Shaddai*. The word *El* means "strong one," while the word *Shaddai* literally means "the breasted." Thus, in this verse, God was describing not only His great strength and absolute power but also His loving care and ability to satisfy all our needs. He was reminding Abraham of the fact that He is all-sufficient; He has the power to bring life to a dead womb.

Likewise, the Lord gave Abram a new name as a confirmation of His promise to him: "Neither shall thy name any more be called Abram ["the exalted father"], but thy name shall be Abraham ["father of a multitude"]; for a father of many nations have I made thee" (v. 5). The Lord also changed Sarai's name to Sarah—a word meaning "princess"—as a token of His promise to make her the mother of kings and nations (see vv. 15,16).

Can you imagine the reaction of Abraham's servants when he told them what God had said? I can just see Abraham lining up his 318 servants (see 14:14) and saying, "Now, men, I want you to know I have a new name. It's no longer Abram, the exalted father; it's Abraham, the father of a multitude." I'm sure some of them snickered and said, "Father of a multitude indeed! He has one son, Ishmael, and he's too old to have any more."

But the "impossible" happened! Abraham and Sarah had a son just as God had promised. Isaac became a great source of joy to them. They realized, as all parents should, that their child was a gift from God—a gift with tremendous potential. They also experienced the joy of true faith in God as they saw the product of their faithfulness.

Like Abraham and Sarah, God wants us to have joy in life—the joy that is the result of faith. While unbelief leads to sorrow, faith leads to joy even in

41

the midst of difficult, impossible circumstances. In Psalm 16:11 we read this promise: "Thou wilt shew me the path of life: in thy presence is fulness of joy; at thy right hand there are pleasures for evermore." However, this doesn't mean that God spares us from all the trials of life. He wants us to learn joy in the midst of those trials. This kind of joy cannot be found in the world or inside ourselves—we must receive it from God. With the Lord's help, we can learn to laugh as we face the impossible.

Laughter of Wonderful Faith

In the story of Isaac we find four different kinds of laughter. First, we see *the laughter of wonderful faith.* Genesis 17:17 states, "Then Abraham fell upon his face, and laughed." Some scholars believe that Abraham's laughter here was the laughter of unbelief. I don't agree with them. I think that Abraham was responding in joyful anticipation; he was filled with joy as he realized what God was going to do for him.

When Abraham was 75 years old, the Lord called him and promised him that through his family all the nations of the earth would be blessed (see 12:1-4). But Abraham and Sarah had no family at the time. Abraham waited ten years for the promised child. When Sarah still did not conceive, she said to Abraham, "Why don't you marry Hagar, my maid, and have a son by her?" (see 16:1-3). Abraham did as Sarah asked, and Hagar conceived and gave birth to Ishmael (see vv. 4,15). I'm sure that Abraham loved Ishmael very much. He was his firstborn and, at that time, his only son.

At the age of 99, Abraham may have begun to think that God was going to fulfill His promise to him through Ishmael. The Lord spoke to Abraham again, confirming His covenant with him that Sarah—not Hagar or any other woman—would bear him the son that would become a great nation. When he heard the Lord's words, Abraham was overwhelmed with joyful, wonderful faith that expressed itself in laughter.

We find a confirmation of this in Romans 4:19-21: "And being not weak in faith, he considered not his own body now dead, when he was about an hundred years old, neither yet the deadness of Sarah's womb: he staggered not at the promise of God through unbelief; but was strong in faith, giving glory to God; and being fully persuaded that, what he had promised, he was able also to perform." I like Romans 4:21. In one verse we see man's *persuasion* of God's *performance* of His *promise*. Instead of looking at himself and his wife, Abraham looked at God and realized that He had the power to do exactly what He said he would do. In a sense, the Lord raised Abraham and Sarah from the dead; His resurrection power was at work in their bodies, giving them new life.

Abraham's experience teaches us that, because God is in control of our lives, no situation is impossible. When we realize this, we can then have the same wonderful faith and joy that Abraham possessed. Of course, we all face impossibilities in our lives. Often God's promises appear to be too long in coming. Many times the Lord's arm seems to be short, or weak. These are the times when we need to take hold of God's promises and just believe what He says. When we do, we will experience the joy and peace that comes from faith in Him. This is what God wants us to enjoy. When we have the joy and peace that comes from believing, we will not be worried about circumstances. We will not worry about our own weakness; instead, we will think only of what God can do. And we will enjoy the laughter of wonderful faith.

Laughter of Shameful Unbelief

While Abraham enjoyed the laughter of wonderful faith, Sarah experienced *the laughter of shameful unbelief.* Shortly after God spoke to Abraham, reaffirming His promise to him, the Lord Jesus and two angels paid a visit to Abraham (see Gen. 18:1-8). "And they said unto him, Where is Sarah thy wife? And he said, Behold, in the tent. And he said, I will certainly return unto thee according to the time of life, and, lo, Sarah thy wife shall have a son. And Sarah heard it in the tent door, which was behind him. Now Abraham and Sarah were old and well stricken in age; and it ceased to be with Sarah after the manner of women. Therefore Sarah laughed within herself, saying, After I am waxed old shall I have pleasure, my lord being old also? And the Lord said unto Abraham, Wherefore did Sarah laugh, saying, Shall I of a surety bear a child, which am old?

Is any thing too hard for the Lord? At the time appointed I will return unto thee, according to the time of life, and Sarah shall have a son. Then Sarah denied, saying, I laughed not; for she was afraid. And he said, Nay; but thou didst laugh" (vv. 9-15).

Surely Sarah knew what God had promised. No doubt, Abraham would have told her what the Lord had said to him. Yet, when she heard the promise for herself, she laughed. Did she doubt God's word? Did she wonder if it could really happen? In this passage we see the tragic consequences of unbelief. Sarah was limiting God's power. The Lord knew what she was thinking and said, "Is any thing too hard for the Lord?" What seemed impossible to Sarah was a simple matter to God.

Like Sarah, we need to remember that we worship the God of the impossible. Nothing is too hard for Him to perform. He has proved this again and again in history. When Job was suffering, the Lord came to him and showed him all He had done in nature. As Job saw God's great power displayed, he cried out, "I know that thou canst do every thing" (Job 42:2). The Prophet Jeremiah also came to this realization. He stated, "Behold, thou hast made the heaven and the earth by thy great power and stretched out arm, and there is nothing too hard for thee" (Jer. 32:17). When the angel Gabriel revealed to Mary that she was to have a child, even though she was a virgin, he added, "For with God nothing shall be impossible" (Luke 1:37). Likewise, Paul realized that he served the God of the impossible. He stated, "Now unto him that is able to do exceed-

45

ing abundantly above all that we ask or think, according to the power that worketh in us, unto him be glory in the church" (Eph. 3:20,21). God is greater than any need or problem we may have.

Sarah laughed because she did not believe that God had the power to overcome her age and barrenness. When the Lord confronted her unbelief, she became afraid. This fear led to deceit. She lied to the Lord, saying, "I didn't laugh" (see Gen. 18:15). Trying to limit God's power is dangerous, for it leads to fear. We become afraid of the future and start to wonder if God really knows what He is doing.

Fortunately for Sarah, she did have faith ultimately. Hebrews 11:11 states, "Through faith also Sara herself received strength to conceive seed, and was delivered of a child when she was past age, because she judged him faithful who had promised." I think once Sarah confessed her sin and she and Abraham began to pray about this matter, her faith started to grow.

Too many people today are laughing in shameful unbelief. I've often heard someone say, "God can't do that. You're a fool to believe He will." I have been involved in some church building programs where unbelieving people have said, "You'll never raise enough money to complete this project. It can't be done." How many times has a doctor told the family of a seriously ill patient, "I'm afraid he is not going to live," only to witness the miraculous healing power of the Lord? God can, and does, perform the impossible. Don't laugh at God! Instead, trust Him in everything, and you will laugh with Him as you see Him work miracles in your life.

Laughter of Joyful Fulfillment

In Abraham and Sarah we have seen two kinds of laughter. Because of his faith in God, Abraham was able to laugh and rejoice with the Lord at the news that he would finally be a father. Sarah, on the other hand, refused to believe and laughed at God. But soon they both discovered a third kind of laughter—*the laughter of joyful fulfillment*—as Isaac was born: "And the Lord visited Sarah as he had said, and the Lord did unto Sarah as he had spoken. For Sarah conceived, and bare Abraham a son in his old age, at the set time of which God had spoken to him. And Abraham called the name of his son that was born unto him, whom Sarah bare to him, Isaac" (Gen. 21:1-3).

Imagine the joy that Abraham and Sarah felt as they held their miracle baby! A joy so great they simply had to laugh aloud. God had done the impossible! He had given a 90-year-old wife and 100-year-old husband a child. I imagine this couple's servants and neighbors probably laughed at them when they said they were going to be parents. But now these same people were laughing *with* Abraham and Sarah: "And Sarah said, God hath made me to laugh, so that all that hear will laugh with me. And she said, Who would have said unto Abraham, that Sarah should have given children suck? for I have born him a son in his old age" (vv. 6,7).

God keeps His promises. He loves us and knows

47

what is best for us. He also knows when the time is right for us to receive it. At His appointed time, He performs it according to His great power. Nowhere is this more evident than in God's messianic plan. God had promised that one day the seed of the woman would crush the head of the serpent (3:15). Through the centuries God's plan slowly unfolded— through Abraham, Isaac, Jacob, the 12 tribes of Israel, David—until Jesus Christ, the Messiah, was born in Bethlehem. And when the time was right, Christ went to the cross and rose again, crushing the power of death and of Satan for good. The Lord kept His promise.

The birth of Isaac was not only an important link in the Lord's ultimate plan for the world, but it pointed the way to the coming Messiah. The joy that Abraham and Sarah felt at the birth of Isaac would pale in comparison to the joy that the Messiah would bring. This is the joy the angels were referring to when they announced: "Fear not: for, behold, I bring you good tidings of great joy, which shall be to all people. For unto you is born this day in the city of David a Saviour, which is Christ the Lord" (Luke 2:10,11).

Sarah and Abraham experienced the laughter of joyful fulfillment. I've often wondered if Abraham was feeling joy over more than just the birth of Isaac. Could he have seen a glimpse of the miraculous birth to come? I think this may have been what Jesus was referring to when He said, "Abraham rejoiced to see my day: and he saw it, and was glad" (John 8:56).

Isaac's life, as well as his birth, is a picture of Christ. Like Jesus, Isaac was willing to put his life on the altar in obedience to his father (see Gen. 22:1-15). Just as Isaac married the bride of his father's choosing (see ch. 24), our Lord is taking His bride, the Church. Isaac was an obedient son until death. And Jesus, the Son of God, was "obedient unto death, even the death of the cross" (Phil. 2:8). Thus, the joy of Abraham was the joy of seeing the Lord Jesus in Isaac.

Laughter of Scornful Envy

We see a fourth kind of laughter displayed in the life of Isaac—*the laughter of scornful envy.* When Isaac had been weaned, Abraham and Sarah held a feast in his honor. Ishmael, then a young man, was jealous of the attention being given to Isaac and began persecuting him. Genesis 21:9 tells us, "And Sarah saw the son of Hagar the Egyptian, which she had born unto Abraham, mocking."

In this verse, the Hebrew word for "mocking" is the one from which the word for "Isaac" comes. It means "a laughter of mocking, a scornful laughter." Rather than laughing with Isaac in celebration of the joyous occasion, Ishmael was laughing at Isaac. He may have been telling the little boy, "So, you think you are so special, do you? Well, I am Father's firstborn son. I'm the rightful heir, not you!" Ishmael was envious of Isaac's special position.

In Ishmael and Isaac we see the conflict between the flesh and the Spirit. Ishmael represents the flesh. He was born of the flesh; he was not a miracle

49

child like Isaac. He was born because of man's will, not God's will. Isaac represents the Spirit. He was born as a direct result of the Spirit's work in the lives of Abraham and Sarah. Throughout the Old Testament, we find God rejecting the firstborn while blessing the second child. He rejected Cain and accepted Abel. Isaac was chosen over Ishmael. God blessed Jacob and gave him Esau's inheritance. In this God is saying to us, "I don't accept your first birth. I only accept a second birth."

Because Ishmael scornfully laughed at Isaac, the Lord told Abraham to send him and his mother away (see vv. 10-12). In the same way, when the flesh and the Spirit are in conflict with each other, God says there cannot be room for both.

What kind of laughter are you enjoying today? Can you laugh because of your wonderful faith? Are you trusting God to do the impossible? If so, then one day you'll experience the laughter of joyful fulfillment. Don't be guilty of laughing in shameful unbelief or scornful envy. This only brings fear and rejection. God has a plan for your life and the power to fulfill it. He is the God of the impossible. He keeps His promises, and He keeps them on time. Rejoice in what He has done, and will do, for you.

Chapter 5

Father Names the Baby

Benjamin

Be careful what name you give to your child, because that name could affect the child for the rest of his or her life. Some years ago, Dr. Robert Nicole made a survey of 15,000 delinquents. He discovered that those with strange names were in trouble with the police four times more often than those who had more acceptable names. In other words, a name affects a child's self-esteem, which in turn affects his or her behavior.

How would you like to bear the name "son of my sorrow" for the rest of your life? How would you feel if your name was a constant reminder to you that your birth helped cause your mother's death? One great man of the Bible almost faced this dilemma. We read in Genesis 35:16-20: "And they journeyed from Bethel; and there was but a little way to come to Ephrath: and Rachel travailed, and she had hard labour. And it came to pass, when she was in hard labour, that the midwife said unto her, Fear not; thou shalt have this son also. And it came to pass, as her soul was in departing, (for she died) that she called his name Benoni: but his father called him Benjamin. And Rachel died, and was buried in the way to Ephrath, which is Bethlehem. And Jacob set a pillar upon her grave: that is the pillar of Rachel's grave unto this day."

With her dying breath, Rachel gave her special son a name that would have been a burden and a shame to him for the rest of his life. Her name, "Benoni," means "son of my sorrow." However, Jacob renamed the baby "Benjamin," a word meaning "son of my right hand." I'm sure Benjamin was grateful to his father for renaming him.

An Answer to a Mother's Prayer

We can learn more from the life of Benjamin than just the importance of choosing our child's name carefully. What do we see when we look at the life of this little baby? To begin with, we see *an answer to a mother's prayer.*

The story of Jacob and Rachel is a familiar one. Jacob loved Rachel dearly. When he was tricked into marrying her sister, Leah, he worked an additional seven years for Laban so he could marry Rachel as well. Leah soon gave birth to four sons, but Rachel remained barren. She wanted to have children so badly. When she couldn't, she became envious of Leah: "And when Rachel saw that she bare Jacob no children, Rachel envied her sister; and said unto Jacob, Give me children, or else I die. And Jacob's anger was kindled against Rachel: and he said, Am I in God's stead, who hath withheld from thee the fruit of the womb?" (Gen. 30:1,2).

When Rachel complained to Jacob, he angrily replied, "I'm not God. I can't give you children." But Rachel had already devised a plan. She told Jacob, "Why don't you marry my maid Bilhah, and she can have children for me" (see v. 3). This was the same plan that Abraham and Sarah used when he married Hagar. She conceived and gave birth to Ishmael. They chose to usurp God's plan, and the result has caused difficulty and sadness to this day. Unfortunately, Jacob did not learn from his grandfather's mistake. He married Bilhah, and they had two sons—Dan and Naphtali (see vv. 4-8).

Even though Leah had four sons already, she felt she had to keep up with Rachel. So she told Jacob, "Why don't you marry my maid Zilpah and have some sons by her for me?" (see v. 9). Jacob did as she asked, and Gad and Asher were born. Instead of trusting God to do something, Rachel and Leah plotted and planned on their own. Their unbelief created a complex family situation that caused much strife and heartache for them, for Jacob and for the children.

A friend of mine likes to say, "Faith is living without scheming." How true that is! When Rachel finally decided to stop scheming and start praying, she saw results: "And God remembered Rachel, and God hearkened to her, and opened her womb" (v. 22). Apparently, Rachel really began to pray fervently about the situation. And God answered her prayer of faith: "And she conceived, and bare a son; and said, God hath taken away my reproach: and she called his name Joseph [a name meanin' "adding"]; and said, The Lord shall add to me another son" (vv. 23,24). In naming Joseph, Rachel was assuming that God would give her another son. The Lord was faithful. He answered Rachel's prayer, and she had another wonderful son—Benjamin. He was an answer to a mother's prayer.

I thank God for praying mothers. As parents, we should be praying constantly, not only for the birth of our children but for every aspect of their lives. As children, we should be thankful to our parents, relatives and others who have prayed for us. And we should strive to be an answer to their prayers.

A Challenge to a Mother's Faith

Not only was the birth of Benjamin a direct answer to Rachel's prayers, but it was also *a challenge to a mother's faith.* While God heard and answered Rachel's prayer, her request was not without its price. Her answered prayer required much pain and difficulty, eventually costing Rachel her life.

Jacob and his family were on a long trip when Rachel's time came to give birth. They had just left Bethel and were on the way to Hebron to visit Isaac, Jacob's father. In Bethel, Jacob had built an altar as the Lord had instructed him. For a number of years, Jacob had been struggling against God, but at Bethel he finally came back to the Lord. A revival had taken place in Jacob's family. When revival takes place, it needs to start with the leader of the home, as it did in this case. Jacob told the family and servants to cleanse themselves by bringing him all their idols and changing their clothes. Jacob then buried the idols under an oak tree before he and his household left for Bethel (see Gen. 35:1-7).

At Bethel, the Lord blessed Jacob and reaffirmed the promise He had made to Abraham, Isaac and Jacob (see vv. 9-15). Since a revival had taken place in Jacob's life, some might think that he would be freed from pain and problems. Many people are preaching this kind of gospel today. They say, "If you'll just get right with God, life will be easy for you." Of course, in many respects life is easier when we belong to Christ. However, this does not mean that we are freed from all problems, trials and sorrows. In fact, Satan will create even more problems for us because of our faith. While we still must face these trials, we don't have to do it alone. The Lord will walk through the fire with us.

Jacob's life bears out this truth. As soon as he experienced this revival, he and his family immediately faced severe testings. First, Rebekah's beloved nurse, Deborah, died (see v. 8). Then Rachel went into labor while they were still traveling. She had an extremely difficult time. While the baby boy arrived safely, Rachel died in childbirth. She gave her life in order that her beloved son could be born.

We can understand Rachel's feelings as she lay dying, for she realized that she would never see her sons grow up. In her anguish, she named the new baby Benoni, "son of my sorrow [trouble]." The years had not been easy for her. She and the man she loved deeply had been deceived by her father,

55

Laban. When Rachel was finally allowed to marry Jacob, she experienced Leah's jealousy because Jacob loved Rachel more than he did Leah. Then she had not been able to give her husband the one thing she wanted most—children. Because of this, there had been rivalry and competition in the home for years. And now that she was finally able to have children, she was not going to live to enjoy them.

Rachel's death was a severe blow to Jacob. As the heartbroken man looked at his new child, he said, "My son is not going to have the name Benoni. I don't want him to go through life being reminded of the sorrow his birth caused. I'm going to name him Benjamin, which means 'the son of my right hand.'" Instead of having a name that would be a burden to him, Benjamin received a name he could be proud of. In the culture of that day, being at the right hand of a person was a great honor. It was a place of power and authority. And even though he was the youngest, Benjamin became his father's favorite son after Jacob thought Joseph had died. He held the position that would have normally been reserved for the eldest son.

When we are facing life's sorrows and burdens, we can approach them in two ways. We can take the path of unbelief and live by our feelings. This is what Rachel did when her faith was challenged. She focused on her sorrow rather than on God. Many people today are like Rachel. Instead of burying their hurts and sorrows, they choose to memorialize them. They constantly dwell on past problems and make their lives miserable as a result. The other path we can take is that of faith. This is what Jacob did. He looked at his situation through the eyes of faith instead of feeling. He claimed God's promise and believed that the Lord was going to work out His will. We can claim a similar promise today: "And we know that all things work together for good to them that love God, to them who are the called according to his purpose" (Rom. 8:28).

When we are seeking to follow the Lord's will, we can be assured that whatever He allows to happen in our lives will be for our ultimate good. He has our best interests at heart. Jeremiah 29:11 tells us, "For I know the thoughts that I think toward you, saith the Lord, thoughts of peace, and not of evil, to give you an expected end." Another translation renders that last phrase, "To give you a future and a hope" (v. 11, NASB). This passage means a great deal to me. It says that God is thinking about us constantly. His plans for us will never be evil. Thus, even in the midst of tears and heartbreak, we can have hope because we know that God will eventually bring some blessing from our sorrow.

Like Jacob and Rachel, we will go through life naming everything either "son of my sorrow" or "son of my right hand." We can choose to memorialize our heartbreak and hurt and, by remembering it, cause ourselves even more pain. Or we can give our problems to God and say, "Lord, I want this to be at Your right hand. I want You to turn my tragedy into triumph, my sorrow into joy and victory." When we do, God will heal our hurts, just as He did Jacob's.

A Blessing to a Needy World

In addition to being an answer to his mother's prayer and a challenge to her faith, Benjamin's life had far-reaching effects for humanity. His life became *a blessing to a needy world*.

When God called Abraham to leave his home and go where He would lead, the Lord also promised him that he would become the father of a great nation (see Gen. 12:1-3). Through his son, Isaac, and his grandson, Jacob, this promise began to be fulfilled. Jacob's 12 sons became the 12 tribes of Israel. God chose the Children of Israel to be a blessing to the whole world. Through them, the world received knowledge of the true God. Through the Israelites, we were given God's written Word, the Bible, and His Living Word, the Lord Jesus Christ.

Rachel's two sons played a key role in the history of Israel. Jacob and his other sons would have died of starvation if Joseph had not saved them. Thus, Joseph saved the people of Israel from extinction. Likewise, Benjamin became a great tribe. Many important people in God's plan for the nation came from the tribe of Benjamin. The Israelites second judge, Ehud, and first king, Saul, were both from this tribe (see Judg. 3:15 and I Sam. 9:1,2). Esther, who saved Israel from annihilation, was also a Benjamite (see Esther 2:5,7). The Prophet Jeremiah came from the territory of Benjamin. Rachel gave the world the two boys who would protect and guard the nation of Israel through their descendants.

58

But the tribe of Benjamin has a place of importance to Christians as well, for the Apostle Paul was also a descendant of Benjamin (see Phil. 3:5). Paul was called by God to preach the Gospel to the Gentiles. Without Paul, the Gospel would have stayed among the Jews, and we would have no hope today. Without Paul, we would not have the last half of the Book of Acts or the important and inspired teachings found in his many letters.

Rachel had no idea what a blessing her sons would be to the world. Likewise, we never know what great things the Lord is going to do with our children when we commit them to His service.

A Picture of Our Saviour

Finally, in the life of Benjamin, we see *a picture of our victorious Saviour.* Several aspects of Benjamin's life closely resemble the life of Jesus Christ. Benjamin was born near Bethlehem, the city where Jesus would enter the world as a baby. If Jesus had not come, Bethlehem would still be known as a place of death—the place where Rachel was buried. Instead, it is now celebrated as a place of birth—the city that gave us our Saviour.

Likewise, the names of Benjamin point out different aspects of Christ's life. Jesus Christ, indeed, was the "son of my sorrow." He was "a man of sorrows, and acquainted with grief" (Isa. 53:3). He felt the same burdens we must bear today, and He knew how to weep. In fact, His sorrow was so great that He took it to the cross. There He bore the

59

entire weight of our sins and sorrows (see v. 4); He made them His very own.

But Christ did not remain the man of sorrows. Like Benjamin, He is also the "son of my right hand." The Lord Jesus Christ ascended to the Father, and He is at His right hand today. Psalm 110:1 tells us, "The Lord said unto my Lord, Sit thou at my right hand, until I make thine enemies thy footstool." While Jesus still feels our sorrows and grief, He has broken their power over us. He is now seated at the Father's right hand—the place of power and authority: "Who being the brightness of his glory, and the express image of his person, and upholding all things by the word of his power, when he had by himself purged our sins, sat down on the right hand of the Majesty on high" (Heb. 1:3). Why did Jesus Christ sit down? Because His work was finished.

We find this truth confirmed in Hebrews 10:11-14. "And every priest standeth daily ministering and offering oftentimes the same sacrifices, which can never take away sins: but this man, after he had offered one sacrifice for sins for ever, sat down on the right hand of God; from henceforth expecting till his enemies be made his footstool. For by one offering he hath perfected for ever them that are sanctified." In the Book of Hebrews—in fact, throughout the New Testament—this emphasis is given. Christ is seated because His work is finished. He accomplished the will of God. And now He's waiting for the day when He will return and conquer His enemies forever.

What do we learn from the life of Benjamin? We learn that God can bring victory out of seeming defeat and life out of death if only we will trust Him. Each trial we endure does not have to be named Benoni, "son of my sorrows." The Lord can help us turn our tragedies into triumph for His glory when we walk by faith and look for the "Son of My right hand."

Chapter 6

Remembering to Forget

Ephraim and Manasseh

Have you ever been abused by your family? Has your boss ever lied about you? Have your friends forgotten you at times? How do you handle these hurts in life? One man in the Bible experienced all of these abuses. He went through some tremendous suffering, and yet he found the secret for having a happy heart. That man, of course, was Joseph.

When you mention the name Joseph, no doubt many different scenes come to mind. You may remember Joseph, the misunderstood brother. His brothers envied and hated him so much that they were ready to kill him. However, a caravan of merchants came along, and so they sold him into slavery instead. Or you may think of Joseph, the faithful worker. He became Potiphar's steward, and God blessed him. Likewise, you will recall Joseph, the suffering prisoner. When he was tempted by Potiphar's wife, he refused to yield to her seduction. So she lied about him, and Potiphar had him thrown into prison. For 13 years Joseph went through the valleys and the mountaintops, through suffering and glory. Finally, at the age of 30, we find Joseph, the wise governor. He interpreted Pharaoh's dream and won his release from prison and a position as the governor of Egypt. As second in command to Pharaoh, the Lord used Joseph to save his family and many others from starvation.

Joseph was indeed a great man. He was misunderstood and envied by his brothers, yet he never stopped loving them. He was mistreated by his boss, yet he remained a faithful worker. He was himself a suffering prisoner, yet he reached out and served his fellow inmates. He was a wise governor, who used his power to help others rather than himself.

What was Joseph's secret for victory in the midst of suffering and adversity? We find his secret in the names he gave to his children. When Joseph was elevated to his position as governor, Pharaoh chose a bride for him. Joseph and his wife had two sons: "And unto Joseph were born two sons before the years of famine came, which Asenath the daughter of Potipherah priest of On bare unto him. And Joseph called the name of the firstborn Manasseh: For God, said he, hath made me forget all my toil, and all my father's house. And the name of the second called he Ephraim: For God hath caused me to be fruitful in the land of my affliction" (Gen. 41:50,51).

Notice that Joseph gave Hebrew names to his sons rather than Egyptian ones. The name "Manasseh" means "causing to forget." The name "Ephraim" means "fruitful." These names reveal Joseph's

63

attitude about everything that had happened to him since coming to Egypt. Instead of harboring anger and resentment, Joseph was instead beginning to see God's purpose for his suffering and was able to forgive those who had wronged him. He had learned three important lessons from his years of suffering and servitude.

The Lesson of Forgetfulness

It's vital that we learn the three lessons Joseph learned from his trials. While Joseph had to discover these truths the hard way—from experience—we need not endure the same suffering. We simply need to learn from his example and apply these lessons to our daily activities.

What are the lessons that Joseph learned? Lesson number one was *the lesson of forgetfulness:* "And Joseph called the name of the firstborn Manasseh: For God, said he, hath made me forget all my toil, and all my father's house" (Gen. 41:51). The years in Egypt had taught Joseph how to forgive and forget.

Of all the people in the Bible, no one had more reason to harbor resentment or to seek revenge than Joseph did. Just think of the way his ten brothers treated him! God told Joseph in two dreams that one day he would be a ruler and that his own brothers would bow before him. When Joseph shared this dream with his brothers, they envied and mocked him (see 37:5-11). Their jealousy soon grew to hatred. One day when Joseph was sent to the field, his brothers saw their chance to get rid of him. They plotted how to murder him but were then convinced by Reuben to put him in a pit instead. No doubt Joseph cried out for deliverance, pleading, "Please don't do this to me! I'm your brother!" But they refused to listen to his pleas. When a band of Midianites came along, they sold Joseph as a slave and watched as he was led away to a foreign country (see vv. 13-28).

Joseph could have also resented the many people in Egypt who had hurt him. The wife of his master, Potiphar, lied about him. And even though Joseph had given many years of faithful service to Potiphar and was his most trusted servant, Potiphar chose to listen to the lies of his wife rather than checking out her story. He had Joseph thrown into prison, where he would have remained for the rest of his life if God had not intervened (see ch. 39). In prison Joseph took care of the other prisoners. He interpreted the dreams of Pharaoh's butler and baker. The butler promised Joseph that if he was released, as Joseph had said, then he would take Joseph's case before Pharaoh. But following his release, the butler forgot all about Joseph for two full years (see ch. 40). If you have ever done favors for people, only to have them forget about you, then you know how Joseph felt.

Where was God during these trials? He was right beside Joseph. And despite his suffering and anguish, Joseph never stopped trusting the Lord. His faith kept him going during the hard times and also helped him to see that harboring resentment would

65

only create more problems. Thus, Joseph was later able to say, "I'm going to name this first boy Manasseh, because God has helped me forget what I've been through and what my father's house has done to me" (see 41:51).

When we begin to dwell on our hurts and to resent those who have wronged us, we are only hurting ourselves. However, we all seem to enjoy dredging up memories of something done to us in the past and licking those old wounds. We waste time thinking about the people who have mistreated us and wondering what God is going to do to avenge us. We need to remember that our hearts are like a garden. The type of fruit we produce depends on the kind of seed we plant. When we plant the seeds of anger, jealousy and resentment, they soon sprout into weeds that choke out the beautiful fruit of the Spirit in our lives. When we harbor resentment toward others, we do not hurt them as much as we hurt ourselves.

Does this mean that we should *never* remember the wrongs that have been committed against us? No. When the Bible speaks about forgetting something, it does not mean that we must completely obliterate it from our minds. This would be impossible to do. In fact, the more you try to forget something, the deeper it will bury itself in your heart and the more trouble it will cause. So how do we learn the lesson of forgetfulness? By doing for others what God has done for us. In Hebrews 8:12 we read: "For I will be merciful to their unrighteousness, and their sins and their iniquities will I remember no more." This is repeated again in Hebrews 10:16,17: "This is the covenant that I will make with them after those days, saith the Lord, I will put my laws into their hearts, and in their minds will I write them; and their sins and iniquities will I remember no more."

In these passages, God is speaking about the sins we have committed against Him. Since the Lord is omniscient and can see the past, present and future, He would be going against His nature if He were to completely blot out the memory of our sins. So what does God mean when He tells us, "I will remember your iniquities and your sins no more"? He is saying, in effect, "I'm not going to hold your sins against you. Of course, I know what sins you've committed; in fact, I know more about your sins than you do. But even though I'll remember what you've done, I will not hold it against you."

When Joseph realized how much God had forgiven him, he was able to follow the Lord's example in forgiving others. Even though Joseph remembered everything he had suffered, he turned these hurts over to God. He said, "My brothers betrayed me, Potiphar and his wife abused me, and the butler forgot me. I have gone through trial and tribulation, but I'm turning it all over to You, Lord. I don't want to hold any of this against these people anymore."

Each of us has a circle of people who have hurt us in some way. What is your reaction when you see these people? Do you immediately remember what they did to you? I hope that you don't hold their sins against them. How should you treat them? Ephe-

67

sians 4:32 tells us, "And be ye kind one to another, tenderhearted, forgiving one another, even as God for Christ's sake hath forgiven you." The British General James Oglethorpe once said to John Wesley, "I never forgive." To this, Wesley wisely replied, "Then, sir, I hope you never sin." While we want others to forgive us, all too often we are unwilling to forgive them. If we do not forgive others, then we should not be surprised when those we have wronged treat us with resentment and hostility.

Joseph was able to overcome any resentment he may have felt because he knew that God was in control. He remembered the dreams the Lord had given to him, and he knew that one day he would be triumphant. He knew that those who had wronged him would eventually bow down to him. Joseph did not live on explanations; he lived on promises. There are no explanations for the injustices of life. No matter how many centuries philosophers and theologians wrestle with this question, they will never be able to explain the inequalities and the hurts of life. But we do not need an explanation; all we need to do is claim the hundreds of promises we find in God's Word.

When we compare ourselves to Joseph, we may be tempted to excuse our actions, saying, "Well, no wonder Joseph could forget the past. He was successful. He had position, wealth and a lovely family. He wasn't still having to deal with his problems." Or we may argue, "We all know that time heals old wounds. Joseph simply had been given enough time to forget." But neither of these statements is true.

When we are harboring resentment and anger, no amount of time or success will cause us to forget.

The only way we can rid ourselves of old hurts is by giving them to God. Paul stated, "This one thing I do, forgetting those things which are behind, and reaching forth unto those things which are before, I press toward the mark for the prize of the high calling of God in Christ Jesus" (Phil. 3:13,14). When we are constantly carrying around old baggage filled with hurt and resentments, our hands and hearts are not free to receive what God wants to give us today. Unless we rid ourselves of the past, it will continue to hinder our Christian walk.

The Lesson of Fruitfulness

Like Joseph, we need to learn the lesson of forgetfulness. In addition, we also need to learn *the lesson of fruitfulness.* When Joseph's second son was born, he named him Ephraim, a name meaning "fruitful." Why did he give him this name? "For God hath caused me to be fruitful in the land of my affliction" (Gen. 41:52).

Notice the sequence of the statements made in Genesis 41:51,52: "God hath made me. . . . God hath caused me." Joseph was a God-made man. The God who created Joseph also placed him in Egypt. And it was his experiences in Egypt that made Joseph into the man he really was. He went into the furnace as a lump of impure metal and came out refined into pure gold. First, God made Joseph into a person He could use, and then He caused him to be fruitful.

If you want to be fruitful in your Christian life, you must first allow God to mold you. How does the Lord do this? Through trial and adversity. We find a perfect illustration of this in nature. In order for a farmer to grow fruit, he must first plow the soil and plant the trees. Then he carefully tends and waters them. Finally, the trees begin to blossom and bear fruit. However, in order for the trees to bear more fruit, the farmer must prune back the branches from time to time. In the same way, the trials that we experience serve to plow up the soil of our soul and prepare it for the seeds God wants to plant. Then, in order for us to reach maturity, we must endure prunings from time to time. We cannot be a fruitful Christian without first undergoing this process of suffering.

The Lesson of God's Faithfulness

Forgetfulness and fruitfulness are the result of God's faithfulness. Often God allows people and circumstances to hurt us so He can teach us *the lesson of faithfulness.* Joseph's years of suffering taught him one important truth: *God is in control.* The Lord enabled him to forget the past and caused him to be fruitful. God was the one who deepened the roots of Joseph's soul and increased his faith.

Too often you and I live by our feelings and by circumstances. Having true faith means we trust God and obey Him in spite of the way we feel and the way our situation looks. When we are living by faith, we do not base our decisions on how we feel at the moment. If Joseph had lived by his feelings, he would have fallen apart. Instead, he trusted the Lord and thus learned the lesson of *God's* faithfulness. Learning the lesson of faithfulness does not mean we must have a great faith—only that we place our simple trust in the great faithfulness of our God.

When Joseph trusted God with his life, the Lord was faithful to work everything for good. While, at the time, Joseph could not see the good that would come from his trials in Egypt, in the end he saw how the Lord had worked through them. Joseph told his brothers, "But as for you, ye thought evil against me; but God meant it unto good" (Gen. 50:20). We find this same truth expressed in Romans 8:28: "And we know that all things work together for good to them that love God, to them who are the called according to his purpose."

How does God help us in our trials so that we are able to forget and to be fruitful? First, He helps us by *His providence*. We may not be able to see how right now, but God is at work in our lives. When we are in the fires of adversity, we may say to ourselves, *I don't see everything working out for good*. But Romans 8:28 doesn't say that we *see* the good; it says that we *know* it.

I would much rather know something than see it. Appearances can often be deceiving. I have seen things that were not there. I recall waking up one night in a hospital room and seeing some things I'd never seen before. But they really weren't there. The medication they had given me was causing me to imagine things. However, when we know something is true, then nothing that we see or experience can shake our faith in that truth. Thus, we can *know* that *all* things are working together for good *now*, even if they don't appear to be.

God's faithfulness is also seen in *His presence* in our lives at all times. The Lord was with Joseph in his trials. Several times in Genesis 39 we are reminded that the Lord was with Joseph (vv. 2,3,21,23). Wherever Joseph was—whether in a pit, a prison or a palace—God was with him. Likewise, we have the Lord's promise: "Lo, I am with you alway, even unto the end of the world" (Matt. 28:20).

We can be comforted in our suffering by the knowledge that God is faithfully working out His plan for our good. We see this by His providence, by His presence with us and by *His provision*. As Joseph cried out to God, the Lord gave him the grace, the patience and the wisdom that he needed to live through—and grow from—his trials. God had promised to give Joseph a throne, and He kept His promise. Joseph knew that God was going to fulfill everything He had said He would do.

You and I know that the cross of Christ made it possible for us to experience forgetfulness, fruitfulness and God's faithfulness. But even Joseph was given a picture of this (see Gen. 48). When he brought his sons to be blessed by his father, Jacob, he arranged it so that Jacob's right hand would be on Manasseh (the firstborn) and his left hand would be on Ephraim (the second born). Instead, Jacob crossed his arms, putting his right hand on Ephraim and his left hand on Manasseh. This reminds us once again that God rejects our first birth but accepts our second birth. And it is the cross that makes a second birth possible.

Are you experiencing difficulties and trials? Have family members, friends or people in your church hurt you? Are you being persecuted because you are serving God? Are these things tempting you to harbor resentment? Before you allow bitterness to take root and poison your soul, learn the lessons God taught Joseph and do what he did. Don't try to manage your problems and feelings by yourself. Don't try to figure out ways to return evil to other people. And don't hide your resentment and anger inside. Instead, turn everything over to God. Confess your sin and forgive those who have wronged you. Then ask God to give you the grace of forgetfulness and the blessing of fruitfulness because of His faithfulness. Then when Satan tries to remind you of your hurts, you will be able to resist the urge to dwell on them because you have already turned them over to the Lord. Once your problems are out of your hands, you can trust God to take care of them. He always keeps His promises.

Chapter 7

The Baby Who Rescued His People

Moses

Each year 125 million babies are born in the world. Ten percent of these children will die before their first birthday. In the history of the Israelites, there was a time when the mortality rate was much higher than this. The Egyptian king issued a decree that every male Hebrew baby born was to be murdered. However, one important baby was protected by God and survived the slaughter. And because he lived to complete God's plan, we have the opportunity today to trust Jesus Christ as our Saviour.

In the centuries between Abraham and Jesus, probably the greatest person in sacred history was Moses. The name Moses is mentioned more than 800 times in the Bible. Moses is revered by Jews, Muslims and Christians alike. When we remember the life of this man, we think of Moses, the great leader, who took a multitude of slaves and molded them into a nation that could serve God. Or we think of Moses, the great lawgiver, through whom God gave His commandments. Or Moses, the deliverer, who pointed the way to Jesus Christ, our Saviour. He was indeed a man used by God.

From birth, it was clear that God's hand was on this special man. We read in Exodus 2:1-10: "And there went a man of the house of Levi, and took to wife a daughter of Levi. And the woman conceived, and bare a son: and when she saw him that he was a goodly [beautiful] child, she hid him three months. And when she could not longer hide him, she took for him an ark of bulrushes, and daubed it with slime and with pitch, and put the child therein; and she laid it in the flags by the river's brink. And his sister stood afar off, to wit [see] what would be done to him. And the daughter of Pharaoh came down to wash herself at the river; and her maidens walked along by the river's side; and when she saw the ark among the flags, she sent her maid to fetch it. And when she had opened it, she saw the child: and, behold, the baby wept. And she had compassion on him, and said, This is one of the Hebrews' children. Then said his sister to Pharaoh's daughter, Shall I go and call to thee a nurse of the Hebrew women, that she may nurse the child for thee? And Pharaoh's daughter said to her, Go. And the maid went and called the child's mother. And Pharaoh's daughter said unto her, Take this child away, and nurse it for me, and I will give thee thy wages. And the woman took the child, and nursed it. And the child grew, and she brought him unto Pharaoh's daughter, and he became her son. And she called his name Moses: and she said, Because I drew him out of the water."

The name Moses is similar to a Hebrew word that means "to draw out of the water." From the life of

Moses, we can learn four important facts about God's work in our own lives. Remembering these facts can encourage and strengthen us as we serve Him.

Born at God's Time

The first encouragement we find in the life of Moses is the fact that he was *born at God's time*. As frail humans, we live within a time frame and are sometimes the victims of time. We regulate our lives by it, and we never seem to have enough time to do everything we want or need to do. God, on the other hand, lives above time. But even though He is not controlled by time, He has chosen to work in the framework of time for our sakes.

However, unlike us, the Lord's timing is always perfect. He is never late in working out His perfect plan. While we often cannot see the purpose for God's bringing something into our lives at a certain time, we can have faith that He has a special reason for it. Thus, the birth of a baby—or some other event—is never an accident; it is an appointment.

The parents of Moses may have wondered about God's timing when their son was born. Moses was born at one of the most difficult times in Jewish history. After the death of Joseph, his family remained in Egypt, where they were treated well for many years. But then a new pharaoh came into power who did not remember Joseph (see Ex. 1:8). He turned against the Jewish people. The Hebrew nation was becoming very large, and the king feared that they would become too strong and would launch a revolt against Egypt. So the Egyptians placed the Hebrew people in bondage. When the Hebrews continued to multiply, the pharaoh decided the only way to solve the problem was to kill the male children. And so he issued an edict that every male Hebrew baby born should be killed. However, the Hebrew midwives refused to obey the edict; they feared and obeyed God instead (see vv. 9-17). Likewise, when Moses was born, his parents refused to allow their precious child to be killed.

It may seem strange to us that God would send this child into the world at a time when baby boys were in such grave danger. But the birth of Moses was no accident. He arrived according to God's appointed time. And the Lord not only spared his life, but He used the special circumstances to work out His perfect plan for delivering the Children of Israel. Only at this time in the history of Israel's bondage in Egypt would it have been possible for a Hebrew slave to be raised as a son of the pharaoh.

God knew every detail of Moses' life before he was even born. The same is true of our lives. Psalm 139:16 is one of the most difficult verses in the Bible to translate. But once we understand it, this passage contains a great promise for us. Dr. H. C. Leupold has translated it this way: "Thy eyes beheld my unformed substance; in thy book it was all written, days which were to be prepared when as yet there was not one of them." Another Hebrew scholar, A. F. Kirkpatrick, translates this verse, "And in thy book were all of them written, even days which were formed when as yet there were none of them." God's eyes are on a baby from the moment of conception. The Lord records every day of that child's life—when he will be born and how long he will live. This is not fatalism; it is the loving plan of a gracious Father for children whom He loves.

Thus, the birth of a baby is an appointment, not an accident. We see examples of this marvelous truth throughout the Bible. Isaac was born at the exact time God appointed, not a moment sooner or later. And even though it was a time of peril, Moses arrived at just the right time in history. Of course, the greatest example is Jesus Christ. The Jews waited centuries for the Messiah to come as God had promised. Many wondered why the Lord delayed so long in coming. But God knew all along when the right time was. And "when the fulness of the time was come, God sent forth his Son" (Gal. 4:4).

Have you ever heard a couple say, "We are planning to wait until times are better before we have children"? Maybe they are waiting until they have more money or more time. Or perhaps they are hoping that the world situation will improve. But, as we have all discovered, there is rarely a good time for a baby to be born! Throughout history, you find people saying, "The world can't possibly get any worse than this." Every period in history has been filled with problems. Likewise, if every couple waited until they had enough money or time to have children, most of us wouldn't be around today!

When we look at the babies of the Bible, we see that none arrived at a really good time. Benjamin certainly didn't arrive at an opportune time for Rachel; he was born on the road, miles from home. The Prophet Samuel was born at a time when the Israelites were at a low level spiritually. And, from a human standpoint, Jesus definitely didn't arrive at a "good" time. His parents were poor. They were living under the iron heel of Rome, and taxes were high. In fact, they were in Bethlehem to pay their taxes when Mary went into labor. Because of the huge crowds, they couldn't even find a room in the inn. Mary had to have her baby in a stable. But all of this took place exactly as God had planned.

Like the Lord Jesus, Moses arrived at a time of peril. But it was also a time of promise. Stephen referred to this when he stated, "But when the time of the promise drew nigh, which God had sworn to Abraham, the people grew and multiplied in Egypt, till another king arose, which knew not Joseph. The same dealt subtilly with our kindred, and evil entreated our fathers, so that they cast out their young children, to the end they might not live. In which time Moses was born" (Acts 7:17-20). Times of peril are also times of promise.

We, too, are living in times of peril. In these difficult days, we need to remember that God's promises are still true. He had a plan long before we were born, and He will see that plan through to completion. Centuries before God called Moses to deliver His people, the Lord told Abraham that his descendants would be in a land of affliction, that they would serve their captors for 400 years and that they would eventually be liberated (see Gen.

79

15:13,14). Joseph also knew that a time of liberation would come. As he was dying, Joseph told his family, "God will surely visit you, and bring you out of this land unto the land which he sware to Abraham, to Isaac, and to Jacob. And Joseph took an oath of the children of Israel, saying, God will surely visit you, and ye shall carry up my bones from hence" (50:24,25). Joseph was so certain that God would lead the people out of Egypt and back to the Promised Land that he left instructions to have the people take his bones with them.

God had His program for Israel planned from the beginning. Moses was born according to God's timetable. In the same way, we are born in God's perfect time, and He is in control of every aspect of our lives. We simply need to trust the Lord and wait for Him to work out His plan for us.

Born With God's Blessing

Not only was Moses born at the time God had ordained, but he was also *born with God's blessing*. In describing Moses, Stephen stated that he was "exceeding fair" (Acts 7:20). Exodus 2:2 adds that he was a "goodly child" (beautiful child). This was more than an outward beauty; Moses was beautiful to God. His mother could tell that there was something very special about Moses as soon as he was born.

The Scriptures also seem to indicate that God somehow revealed to Moses' parents the fact that he would be no ordinary child. Hebrews 11:23 states, "By faith Moses, when he was born, was hid

80

three months of his parents, because they saw he was a proper child; and they were not afraid of the king's commandment." This passage is not discussing the faith of Moses. Rather it is referring to the faith of his parents, Amram and Jochebed. They believed that God's special blessing was upon Moses. By faith, they committed their child to God, and the Lord protected both Moses and his parents.

I believe that every child who comes into this world can be used by God in a wonderful way. Of course, we won't all be a Moses or a Samuel; however, we can all serve God in our way. Every time a child is dedicated to God, I often think, *I wonder if this baby is going to be the next great evangelist or missionary. Will this child grow up to be a wonderful father or mother who will raise his children to serve the Lord?* When you commit your children to the Lord, He will bless them and use them greatly.

Moses was born at God's time, and he was born with God's blessing. Moses was very fortunate to have believing parents who entrusted him to God for His glory, parents who believed God in spite of the circumstances and who were even willing to defy the king in order to follow His plan. Many of us have the same kind of parents. How long has it been since you thanked your parents for their faith and commitment?

Born to God's Service

The third important fact we learn about the life of Moses is that he was *born to God's service.* He was rescued from the Nile River in order to serve God as the deliverer for the Children of Israel. After hiding the baby for three months, Moses' parents placed him in a reed basket and set him afloat on the river. They left him completely in the care and providence of God. And, according to God's plan, Pharaoh's daughter found Moses and adopted him. "And she called his name Moses: and she said, Because I drew him out of the water" (Ex. 2:10).

I'm sure that Moses' name was an encouragement to him many times during his life. Every time he found himself in a difficult situation, he may have thought, *My name is Moses. God drew me out of the water, and He will draw me out of this situation.* When Moses was disheartened, no doubt God used his name to encourage him. It reminded him that he served a God of redemption, a God who loved him enough to reach down and pull him out of the water.

David also knew what it was like to have the Lord rescue him from difficulties. In Psalm 18:16 David used the same Hebrew word from which the name Moses is derived. He said, "He sent from above, he took me, he drew me out of many [great] waters." When David was drowning in trouble, the Lord had reached down and lifted him out of the deep waters of despair. He does the same for us.

Just as God drew Moses out of the water of the Nile, He used Moses to draw the people out of Egypt and to lead them through the desert. In the wilderness when the people were hungry and thirsty, when they were facing battles and uncrossable seas, God lifted them out of their troubles.

Moses had been born for God's service, and the Lord used him again and again to accomplish His purposes. While God may not use us to part the waters of a raging river or to lead a multitude of people, He does call each of us to serve Him in some way. And He also equips us for that service.

Born for God's Glory

Finally, the life of Moses teaches us that he was *born for God's glory.* Whenever we think about God's glory being revealed, we imagine some great and miraculous act. However, God frequently uses the weak and simple things of this world to bring glory to Himself. In I Corinthians 1:27-29 we read: "But God hath chosen the foolish things of the world to confound the wise; and God hath chosen the weak things of the world to confound the things which are mighty; and base things of the world, and things which are despised, hath God chosen, yea, and things which are not, to bring to nought things that are: that no flesh should glory in his presence."

We find a perfect illustration of this in the life of Moses. The contrasts in Exodus 2:1-10 are amazing. Egypt was the most powerful country in the world during this time in history. They had a vast empire, huge armies and magnificent pyramids that are still an architectural wonder today. This country possessed all the power, authority and pride they could want. Because they were mistreating God's people, the Lord was about to judge this great empire. Yet how did He do it? He sent a tiny Hebrew baby born into a simple Jewish family.

83

Have you ever noticed that whenever God wants to accomplish something, He sends a baby? He didn't send an army; He sent a baby. The mighty pharaoh, whose words alone could take someone's life, was unable to destroy this baby. This baby's tears melted the heart of Pharaoh's daughter and overcame an entire country. This baby was greater than the gods of the Egyptians. Egypt depended on the Nile River and worshiped it as a god. When Pharaoh commanded the boy babies to be thrown into the river, it was the same as giving them to this god. But Moses was rescued from the water of the Nile. God didn't use thunderbolts or a great army to accomplish His plan. Instead, He sent a tiny, crying baby, who was marked for death, to conquer the great empire of Egypt.

Contrary to what some people might think, Egypt was not defeated by the plagues. It was conquered because of a tiny, weak, weeping baby, who was rescued and raised by the enemy. God used Moses to bring redemption to His people. Pharaoh thought he was so wise. He devised a plot to destroy the Hebrews, but God used his own "foolish" plot to destroy Egypt. When we try to live by our wisdom, we are sure to fail, for the wisdom of this world is foolishness to God.

Why does God use the foolish and weak things of the world to achieve His purposes? So that "no flesh should glory in his presence" (I Cor. 1:29). God does not want us to glory in our own strength and wisdom. When we are weak, we rely totally on the strength of God. Thus, when we see great things happening, we realize that God is at work in us and give Him the glory He deserves.

Moses was born according to God's perfect timing. He was born with God's blessing and for His service. And the Lord used Moses for His honor and glory. The same can be true of us when we willingly submit to God's plan for our lives.

Chapter 8

Help for a Stranger

Gershom and Eliezer

While many of the names found in the Bible are still popular today—Adam, David, Matthew, John, Mary—few parents are likely to choose the names Gershom or Eliezer for their children. The likelihood of a son's receiving these names is small, not because the parents think these names are bad or because they've never heard of them. It may just be that they have forgotten what these names really mean.

Even though parents may not use these two names, knowing what they mean can help us greatly as we walk with the Lord and seek to serve Him. What do the names Gershom and Eliezer mean? We read in Exodus 18:1-4: "When Jethro, the priest of Midian, Moses' father in law, heard of all that God had done for Moses, and for Israel his people, and that the Lord had brought Israel out of Egypt; then Jethro, Moses' father in law, took Zipporah, Moses' wife, after he had sent her back, and her two sons; of which the name of the one was Gershom; for he said, I have been an alien in a strange land: and the name of the other was Eliezer; for the God of my father, said he, was mine help, and delivered me from the sword of Pharaoh."

When Moses was 40 years old, he killed an Egyptian taskmaster who was beating a Hebrew slave. As a result, he was forced to flee from Egypt. After wandering in the wilderness, he was led to Midian, where he spent the next 40 years (see Ex. 2:11-22; Acts 7:23-30). He married Zipporah, the daughter of Jethro, and they had two sons. The names Moses chose for his sons reflected the experiences he had been through. Exodus 2:22 states, "And she bare him a son, and he called his name Gershom: for he said, I have been a stranger in a strange land." The name Gershom means "sojourner," "alien" or "stranger." The name Eliezer means "God is my help." Moses realized that God was at work in his life. The Lord had saved him as a baby. He had enabled him to escape from Egypt and had taken care of him when he had wandered in the desert and had ultimately led him to the house of Jethro in Midian. But Moses also knew that he was only a temporary visitor to Midian. God had other plans for him.

A Difficult Position

Moses' experiences during his life taught him a great deal about the God he served and about himself. He learned many important lessons, and the names he gave to his sons reflect some of the truths he learned. By examining these names closely, we can also learn from them the lessons

God wants to teach us. The name Gershom reminds us, first of all, of *our difficult position in this world.*

Our Position

As Christians, *we are strangers in this world* because we belong to another world. We have experienced a new birth; therefore, we are no longer true members of this society. Instead, we belong to the heavenly world. In Philippians 3:20 Paul stated that our citizenship is in heaven. A person's citizenship is determined by his birth; since we have had a heavenly birth, we are citizens of heaven.

In John 3:7 our Lord said to Nicodemus, "Ye must be born again." The Greek word translated "again" in this passage also means "from above." Thus, Jesus was saying that we must be born from above. When a person is born the first time, he is born from beneath—in an earthly situation. He is born a child of Adam. However, the second birth is always a heavenly one. We are born again as a child of God; He is our Heavenly Father. Our citizenship is in heaven, our birth is from heaven, our Father is in heaven, and our names are written down in heaven. In Luke 10:20 the Lord told His disciples, "Rejoice, because your names are written in heaven." God is keeping a roll of His citizens, and every person who has accepted Christ as his Saviour has his name written there in God's book.

Because we are citizens of heaven rather than of earth, our priorities and goals should be focused on heaven. Jesus instructed us, "Lay not up for yourselves treasures upon earth. . . . But lay up for yourselves treasures in heaven" (Matt. 6:19,20). Possessions, wealth or fame are temporary; only what we do for Jesus will last. For this reason, we should seek only the things that will reap heavenly rewards. Our future is in heaven. We should continually be looking for Christ's return and living as though He will come back at any moment.

However, this does not mean that we should be so heavenly minded that we are no earthly good. We are seated with Christ in the heavenlies (Eph. 2:6), but we must walk on the earth. And this is a difficult position to be in. We are strangers and aliens in this world. In greeting the churches of Asia, the Apostle Peter wrote: "Peter, an apostle of Jesus Christ, to the strangers scattered throughout Pontus, Galatia, Cappadocia, Asia, and Bithynia" (I Pet. 1:1). The early Christians realized that they were no longer citizens of their countries. They were merely pilgrims on their way to a better place. They could also be called sojourners, as we see from verse 17: "And if ye call on the Father, who without respect of persons judgeth according to every man's work, pass the time of your sojourning here in fear."

Like a person who moves to a foreign country, once we become a Christian, the practices and customs of the world should become strange to us. If the ways of the world are still all too familiar, then we are probably not living as we should. On the other hand, because we are still confined to our imperfect bodies, our old earthly nature will continue to wrestle with our new heavenly one. We will be in a constant battle with ourselves and with the world. In I Peter 2:11,12, Peter urged, "Dearly beloved, I beseech you as strangers and pilgrims, abstain from fleshly lusts, which war against the soul; having your conversation honest among the Gentiles [unbelievers]: that, whereas they speak against you as evildoers, they may by your good works, which they shall behold, glorify God in the day of visitation." We should be living in a way that demonstrates to unbelievers that we do not belong to their world. Of course, when we do not participate in the activities of the world, we will experience persecution.

Our Destination

As strangers and pilgrims, we no longer have the same position in the world that we once had. Likewise, *our destination is now different*. We are now following in the footsteps of people such as Abraham, Isaac and Jacob. In describing Abraham, Hebrews 11:9,10 states, "By faith he sojourned in the land of promise, as in a strange country, dwelling in tabernacles with Isaac and Jacob, the heirs with him of the same promise: for he looked for a city which hath foundations, whose builder and maker is God." The same passage later adds, "These all died in faith, not having received the promises, but having seen them afar off, and were persuaded of them, and embraced them, and confessed that they were strangers and pilgrims on the

90

earth" (v. 13). What kept Abraham, Isaac, Jacob, Joseph, Moses and all the other heroes of the faith going? They were living as strangers and pilgrims. They were singing, "This world is not my home, I'm just apassing through." Even though they had not received what was promised, they could see it through the eyes of faith.

You can always tell the difference between a visitor and a citizen in a country. The stranger is usually talking about heading for some other place. Likewise, you can always recognize one of God's aliens. His eyes are fixed on the future, not on the past. His heart is already in his future home.

Jesus Christ has called us out of this world. Because Christ was not of the world, He was rejected and persecuted. As strangers and sojourners with him, we can expect the same treatment. Jesus told us, "I have given them thy word; and the world hath hated them, because they are not of the world, even as I am not of the world" (John 17:14). Notice Jesus didn't say that we're not *in* the world; He said that we're not *of* the world. Even though we have been called out of this world, we have been left here for now to witness to the world. John 17:18 tells us, "As thou hast sent me into the world, even so have I also sent them into the world." What was our Lord's purpose for leaving us here? "Neither pray I for these alone, but for them also which shall believe on me through their word" (v. 20). Our purpose for being here is so that others can come to know the Lord.

We share Christ with others by more than just

our words. The world watches us; therefore, we must be an example to them. Even though we must live in this world, we should not be taking part in the activities of the world. Our behavior should speak well of our faith. Because we are different, we will be slandered and abused by unbelievers. However, in the end, they will glorify God because our good works have been a testimony to them (see I Pet. 2:11,12). The world hates us, the world watches us, and the world needs us. That's why we're here.

Of course, it's not easy to be a stranger and pilgrim in this world. Because the world's followers hate us, they will continually try to convince us to conform to their standards. Paul felt this pressure. He warned us, "Be not conformed to this world: but be ye transformed by the renewing of your mind" (Rom. 12:2). The world will try to trap us and to use us, but we can overcome these pressures if we remember that life is not a destination—it is a journey. We are merely passing through life on our way home.

The Christian life is not a parking lot; it's a launching pad. As pilgrims and strangers, we should always be on the move. Even though Abraham was a wealthy man, he spent his entire life living in a tent. Wherever Abraham went, he pitched his tent and built an altar. The tent was a reminder to himself and others that he was a pilgrim. Likewise, the altar was a reminder and a witness that he worshiped the true and living God.

As Christians, we should never become too comfortable in the world. The Lord has not left us here merely to enjoy what life has to offer while we wait for Him to return. Everything we have—our body, money, possessions—comes from the Lord. He uses the resources of the world to provide our needs and to equip us for service. However, we need to remember that these things are only temporary. Our body and our possessions are merely tools we use in completing our journey. "For we know that if our earthly house of this tabernacle were dissolved, we have a building of God, an house not made with hands, eternal in the heavens" (II Cor. 5:1). Our physical body is simply a tent that temporarily houses our soul and spirit. When Christ returns, we will receive a glorified body that will last for eternity.

The name Gershom reminds us of our difficult position in this world. We are aliens and strangers. We don't belong to the world; therefore, the world hates us because we're different. To us, life is merely a journey, a place we must travel through to reach our destination—the holy city where Jesus Christ is the light and the king (see Rev. 21:23).

It is important to remember that we are strangers and pilgrims in this world—not vagabonds or fugitives. A vagabond has no home, and a fugitive is always running from home. However, a stranger is merely away from home for a time, and a pilgrim is on the way home. You and I are not fugitives running away from anything. We're not vagabonds wandering around. We are strangers and pilgrims who are on the way home. Because we know where we are going and have God's Word to light the path

93

before us (see Ps. 119:105), we can move confidently toward our destination.

Our Adequate Provision

Of course, God does not ask us to make this journey alone. The name Eliezer reminds us that "God is my help." The Lord has given us *adequate provision* for our pilgrim journey.

We need God's help to find our way in this world. We have many battles to fight and many burdens to carry. Sometimes we wonder if we are really going to survive our journey. Maybe it seems too long or too great to us. It's at these times that we need to remember where our help comes from. If we try to depend on ourselves or on others for strength, we are sure to fail. We must allow God's Word to be the compass that guides us on our pilgrim journey. Without the Lord's help, we will be unable to maintain our separation in this world.

When we are in trouble, God does more than just *send* help—He *is* our help. Of course, the Lord does send help in various ways. Sometimes, unknown to us, He sends His angels to protect us and to accomplish His will for us. Sometimes He sends another Christian to help us. Or maybe He uses a letter or a check. But, in everything, God makes His presence felt in our lives. He realizes that we desire more than solutions to our problems—we are looking for people to help us. When we need to see a doctor, we want a real person to feel our pulse and check our temperature. If we are involved in an auto accident, we don't want a law book—we want a lawyer who knows how to settle our problem to the glory of God. When we have a problem with a computerized bill or statement, we don't want to talk to a machine. We want to see the person in charge. In the same way, God helps us personally and completely.

How do we receive God's help in our lives? Psalm 27:8,9 tells us, "When thou saidst, Seek my face; my heart said unto thee, Thy face, Lord, will I seek. Hide not thy face far from me; put not thy servant away in anger: thou hast been my help; leave me not, neither forsake me, O God of my salvation." When we seek God's help and place our lives in His hands, He will always be there to help us. David discovered this and was later able to say, "The Lord is my strength and my shield; my heart trusted in him, and I am helped: therefore my heart greatly rejoiceth; and with my song will I praise him. The Lord is their strength, and he is the saving strength of his anointed" (28:7,8; see also 30:10).

When we cry out to God, He will help us. He may change our situation, or He may change us so we can deal with our situation. No matter what His answer is, He will give us the grace we need. However, we must also be willing to wait for Him: "Our soul waiteth for the Lord: he is our help and our shield. For our heart shall rejoice in him, because we have trusted in his holy name" (33:20,21). God doesn't always work in our time and in our way. But when we trust the Lord, pray to Him and wait for Him, we will be able to rejoice in Him: "Because thou hast been my help, therefore in the shadow of

95

thy wings will I rejoice" (63:7). Notice that David was not rejoicing in the problems that were solved, but in God, who had provided the answers.

Often we may not think that God is close to us, but He is always near. Psalm 46:1 assures us, "God is our refuge and strength, a very present help in trouble." In our times of trouble, God hides us and helps us. He will not allow us to be moved (v. 5). He has promised to be with us always (Matt. 28:20). We have His word that He will never leave us or forsake us (Heb. 13:5). "Let us therefore come boldly unto the throne of grace, that we may obtain mercy, and find grace to help in time of need" (4:16).

As pilgrims and strangers, we are in a difficult position in this world. Many times our journey through life will be filled with obstacles and trials. People will persecute and hurt us. However, we shouldn't be afraid or discouraged, for our provision is more than adequate for our needs. God is beside us every step of the way. When we place our hand in His and trust Him in everything, He will lead us safely home.

Chapter 9

Babies, the Gift of God

Samuel

If you could choose one skill for your children to master, what skill would you select? Would you select some physical ability, such as athletic prowess? Or would you choose intellectual aptitude—the ability to study and master various subjects? Perhaps you are most concerned that your children know the social skills—how to make and keep friends, how to get along with others, how to perform their jobs well, how to express their feelings. Or maybe you want your children to have financial skill above all so that they can make enough money to retire early and enjoy life.

While many of these skills are desirable or even necessary, I believe one ability stands above them all. This one skill can help our children obtain everything they need in life. What is the greatest skill our children can learn? The ability to pray. When a person knows how to pray, he has the answer to every problem. He knows how to solve every difficulty and to meet every need. He can defeat every enemy. Praying people have character. They know how to serve the Lord. Because they are in constant communion with God and are open to His leading, He can use them.

But like any skill, the ability to pray in God's will is not something we can do naturally. Learning how to pray so that God will answer involves a great deal of time and meditation in His Word.

Of all the great men and women of prayer in the Bible, possibly none exemplifies the ability to pray more than Samuel. The story of Samuel is bathed in prayer. Not only was Samuel a powerful prayer warrior, but also his very existence was a direct answer to prayer. By examining the life of Samuel, we can learn some of the secrets of mastering the skill of prayer and in turn teach these to our children.

Born Through Prayer

What was the relationship of Samuel's life to this matter of prayer? First, we see that Samuel was *born through prayer*. His birth was a direct answer to the prayers of his mother, Hannah. Like Rachel, Hannah was loved dearly by her husband (Elkanah). However, she had been unable to give him children. Elkanah also had another wife who had given birth to many sons and daughters. This provoked Hannah even more. Each year when the family went to the tabernacle in Shiloh to worship and sacrifice, Hannah would be reminded again of her barrenness. She would weep and refuse to eat (see I Sam. 1:1-7).

We find in I Samuel 1 the first *recorded* prayer by

a woman in the Bible. It's a silent prayer. She didn't pray aloud, but we know what she said. When Hannah began to pray for a son, she did it with bitterness at first (v. 10). As she prayed, she made a vow: "O Lord of hosts, if thou wilt indeed look on the affliction of thine handmaid, and remember me, and not forget thine handmaid, but wilt give unto thine handmaid a man child, then I will give him unto the Lord all the days of his life, and there shall no razor come upon his head" (v. 11). Soon her bitterness would be turned into blessedness and her weeping into rejoicing, as the Lord would honor her fervent prayer and vow.

Samuel was very fortunate to have a praying mother. Even when Hannah was facing some difficult circumstances and misunderstandings, this didn't stop her from praying. No doubt her situation at home was difficult. The guilt and depression she felt because of her barrenness was aggravated by the presence of the other wife, Peninnah, and her children. Peninnah may also have taunted Hannah with the fact that she could give Elkanah children while Hannah couldn't.

In addition, Hannah was not living at an easy time in history. It was a time of transition between the period of the judges and the institution of a king. The nation was divided politically. The Philistines were hovering, waiting to attack. The Israelites were in danger. Spiritually, the nation was in sad shape. We read in I Samuel 3:1: "And the word of the Lord was precious [rare] in those days; there was no open [frequent] vision." God was not reveal-

99

ing Himself to His people. Their worship was based on dead tradition. In addition, Eli the priest was not a godly man (2:27-36). His sons were wicked and dishonest (v. 12). Even though the world into which he would be born was dangerous and evil, Hannah still desperately wanted to have a son.

I've heard some couples say, "The world today is so bad that we wouldn't even consider bringing a child into it." However, for all we know, that child could be the instrument God will use to make the world better. As we will see later, Samuel became the answer to Israel's problems. God heard Samuel's prayer for the nation and gave the Israelites victory over the Philistines (see ch. 7). Samuel's prayers united the nation and renewed their dedication to God (see chs. 8-12).

Couples also sometimes view children as a hindrance to their happiness. But parents should never consider their children to be a burden. Instead, they should see them as a blessing from God. Psalm 127:3 tells us, "Lo, children are an heritage of the Lord: and the fruit of the womb is his reward." It seems ironic that we find so many people in the Bible *praying for* children, while today's society is *preying on* innocent children. Children today are living in a dangerous world. We hear of so many who are being kidnapped or abused by parents and other relatives or used for pornography and other sins. Television ads and programs take advantage of their open, receptive minds in order to make a profit. Like Hannah, many people today are begging God to give them children, while millions of others are murdering their children by abortion. Blessed is the child who is wanted and prayed for continually. Blessed is the child who is born into a home that believes in prayer.

When circumstances are difficult and it seems as if our prayers are not being answered, we have a tendency to quit praying. However, those are the times when we need to pray even more. Hannah could have become discouraged. No doubt she had been praying for years that God would enable her to conceive. Yet, even in her bitterness, she never stopped praying. She didn't even stop when she was misunderstood by the priest. When Eli the priest saw Hannah praying silently, he mistakenly thought she was drunk and rebuked her (see I Sam. 1:13,14). Hannah replied, "No, my lord, I am a woman of a sorrowful spirit: I have drunk neither wine nor strong drink, but have poured out my soul before the Lord" (v. 15). When was the last time you prayed so intensely for your children or another burden that your actions were misunderstood?

Hannah was faithful and fervent in her prayers. God honored her request, and Samuel was born. When God's children pray sincerely, faithfully and expectantly in His will, He answers those prayers in marvelous ways.

Named From Prayer

Samuel was born because of the prayers of his mother. In addition, he was also *named from prayer*. In I Samuel 1:20 we read: "Wherefore it came to pass, when the time was come about after

Hannah had conceived, that she bare a son, and called his name Samuel, saying, Because I have asked him of the Lord."

When Hannah conceived shortly after praying to the Lord at Shiloh, she realized that God had indeed answered her prayers. She knew that this baby was a special gift from Him. She chose a name that reflected this truth. The name Samuel means "heard of God" or "asked of God" in the Hebrew language. Every time Samuel heard his name, he would have been reminded that he was the result of answered prayer. This was probably an encouragement to him many times during his difficult ministry. It is no wonder that Samuel became a powerful man of prayer. He was born and named because of prayer. He knew what God would do when His people prayed.

Samuel is a living witness to us today that God answers prayer. When we are faced with difficult times, heavy burdens or pressing decisions, we can remember the name "Samuel" and realize that God will hear and answer our prayers as well.

Nurtured by Prayer

While it is important to pray for the gift of children and to thank God when He answers that prayer, it is even more vital that our children are *nurtured by prayer*. Notice that when Samuel was born, Hannah didn't stop praying. In fact, she probably prayed for him even more fervently.

After the birth of Samuel, Hannah fulfilled the vow she had made to the Lord. She had promised

God that if He gave her a child, she would dedicate him to the Lord's service. Thus, when her son was old enough, Hannah weaned him and took him to Eli the priest. She said, "For this child I prayed; . . . therefore also I have lent him to the Lord; as long as he liveth he shall be lent to the Lord" (I Sam. 1:27,28). After Hannah had worshiped God in the tabernacle, she left Samuel with Eli to be trained for service.

Hannah gave Samuel completely to the Lord. Often many people do not realize the impact of Hannah's vow. In the Old Testament, the tribe of Levi was chosen by God for full-time service in His house. But the Levites were only required to serve for 25 years. They began at the age of 25 and retired at 50. Likewise, many men took the Nazarite vow to serve God. They did not shave and ate only certain foods as part of their commitment. Normally, those who had taken this vow were bound only for a short time. The usual length was 30 days. But the vow sometimes lasted as long as 100 days. Hannah did what few before her had done—she dedicated Samuel to the Lord for life.

Any parent knows how difficult it would have been for Hannah to leave her child behind. Not only had she waited so long to have this baby, but she also knew that Eli was not a faithful priest and that his sons were even more unfaithful. No doubt she was worried about the influence they would have on Samuel. I'm sure that Hannah prayed for Samuel daily, asking God to protect him from evil.

Like Hannah, we should willingly and wholly dedicate our children to the Lord and then surround them daily with prayer. We can't isolate our children from reality or from the sins and temptations of this life, nor should we try to. However, we can fortify and protect them with our prayers so they will have the strength to overcome these evil influences in their lives.

Once Hannah gave Samuel completely to the Lord, she did not try to hold on to him. She allowed him to grow. Each year Hannah visited Samuel and brought him a new coat (2:19). We read in I Samuel 2:21: "And the child Samuel grew before the Lord." What a wonderful way to grow! Verse 26 adds, "And the child Samuel grew on, and was in favour both with the Lord, and also with men." In God's hands, Samuel's growth closely resembled that of the Lord Jesus (see Luke 2:52). He developed a balanced life and was living for the Lord in every way—physically, intellectually, socially and spiritually.

I'm grateful for mothers and fathers who permit their children to grow. They realize that their children will not remain babies, and they do not try to keep them as such. Instead, they raise them in the admonition of the Lord and nurture them with prayer.

Powerful in Prayer

Because Samuel was born through prayer, named from prayer and nurtured by prayer, he became *powerful in his prayer life*. No doubt the example of Hannah had a profound effect on Samuel. He saw the importance and power of prayer in her life and learned to emulate it in his own.

As a result, Samuel became known in the Bible as one of the great prayer warriors. Psalm 99:6 states, "Moses and Aaron among his priests, and Samuel among them that call upon his name; they called upon the Lord, and he answered them." Jeremiah 15:1 adds, "Then said the Lord unto me, Though Moses and Samuel stood before me, yet my mind could not be toward this people: cast them out of my sight, and let them go forth." In these passages Samuel is classified with Moses as a powerful man of prayer. God's words to Jeremiah indicate the impact their prayers had, as well as the depth of Israel's sin. The Lord told Jeremiah, in effect, "Even if Moses and Samuel pleaded with Me in the people's behalf, I would not change the judgment that I have decreed for them." Samuel is also listed in Hebrews 11 among the great heroes of the faith (see v. 32).

Samuel is remembered as a great man of prayer. When people look back and review your life, what will they remember most about you? Will they say, "Bill had such a great sense of humor" or "Jane was a wonderful cook"? I wonder if any of us will be remembered as people of prayer. The Body of Christ desperately needs prayer warriors today.

Samuel was a judge who solved problems through prayer. As you read I Samuel, you will discover that he solved his problems spiritually. He knew how to wage spiritual warfare. The other judges used armies and swords to accomplish the Lord's will.

But Samuel used the sword of the Spirit—the Word of God—and prayer to build the nation and protect it from its enemies.

In I Samuel 3 you find the first prayer of a child in the Bible. Samuel could have been a young teenager by this time. He was asleep when the Lord spoke to him three times. Each time Samuel thought Eli was calling him. After Samuel had come to Eli for the third time, the priest realized that the Lord was speaking to Samuel. He told Samuel to go back and wait for the Lord to speak again (see vv. 1-9). Finally, "the Lord came, and stood, and called as at other times, Samuel, Samuel. Then Samuel answered, Speak; for thy servant heareth" (v. 10). This is the first prayer of Samuel recorded in the Bible.

Samuel's first prayer teaches us one important secret of prayer: *Prayer involves two-way communication.* If we expect the Lord to hear and answer our prayers, we must be open and willing to listen to Him. When we say to God, "Speak, Lord, for Thy servant heareth," one day He will say to us, "Speak, servant, for thy Lord heareth." Samuel waited patiently for the Lord to speak, and God revealed to him the judgment that would take place as well as the blessings that would come (see vv. 11-14). Likewise, our prayers should be more than a list of requests. We should also say to God, "Tell me what You want me to know, Lord" and then open our minds and hearts to receive His Word.

Samuel followed this pattern of prayer throughout his life. When the Philistines were preparing to attack the nation of Israel, the people came to Samuel and said, "Cease not to cry unto the Lord our God for us, that he will save us out of the hand of the Philistines" (7:8). Samuel prayed for his people, and God defeated the enemy.

When Samuel was experiencing disappointments and heartaches, the first thing he did was pray. In I Samuel 8, the people came to the old judge and asked for a king. They no longer wanted Samuel to judge them, and this broke his heart. But more importantly, Samuel could see all the problems that would come from having a king. He prayed to the Lord to learn what he should do (see v. 6). Likewise, when the nation was rededicated to the Lord, Samuel called the people together and prayed for them (see ch. 12). He showed the people the power of prayer. When Samuel prayed, God sent thunder and rain to show that He indeed answers prayer (v. 18). The people feared the Lord and begged Samuel to pray for them (v. 19). Samuel responded, "As for me, God forbid that I should sin against the Lord in ceasing to pray for you" (v. 23). And when King Saul failed so miserably, Samuel prayed all night for him (see 15:11).

Samuel was a man who was born through prayer, named from prayer, nurtured by prayer and powerful in prayer. He was successful and blessed during his life—and beyond—because he mastered the skill of prayer. The greatest blessing parents can give to their children is prayer. We should constantly be saying to our children, "God forbid that I should sin against the Lord in ceasing to pray for you" (12:23). When we set the example as praying parents, nurturing and instructing our children in prayer, we will in turn receive the greatest blessing a parent can know—the blessing of a praying child.

Chapter 10

Babies, an Answer to Prayer

John the Baptist

One of the most familiar names in the Bible continues to be popular today. In fact, this name ranks third in Nebraska as the most widely used boy's name. Many important men in history, including church history, had this name. All of us have acquaintances with this name. This name, of course, is John.

The last—and greatest—of the Old Testament prophets was a man commonly known as John the Baptist. He was sent from God for the express purpose of preparing the way for the Lord Jesus Christ. In addition, he was an answer to the prayers of his parents, Zacharias and Elisabeth. Like Abraham and Sarah, this couple was well past childbearing age and still had no children (see Luke 1:5-7).

Zacharias was a priest and served God faithfully in the temple. One day as he was burning incense and praying for the people, an angel appeared to him (see vv. 8-11). The angel told him, "Fear not, Zacharias: for thy prayer is heard; and thy wife Elisabeth shall bear thee a son, and thou shalt call his name John. And thou shalt have joy and gladness; and many shall rejoice at his birth. For he shall be great in the sight of the Lord. . . . And many of the children of Israel shall he turn to the Lord their God. And he shall go before him in the spirit and power of Elias, . . . to make ready a people prepared for the Lord" (vv. 13-17). This elderly couple had been praying for a child, and now their prayers were being answered. Not only would they have a son in their old age, but this child would be used by God to prepare the people for the coming Messiah. They were being given one of the greatest honors ever bestowed by God.

Elisabeth conceived and gave birth to a son just as the angel had predicted. According to the Jewish custom, the parents brought the baby to the temple on the eighth day to be circumcised. Those present assumed that he would be named Zacharias after his father (see vv. 57-59). But Elisabeth answered, "Not so; but he shall be called John" (v. 60). They did not believe her and tried to ask Zacharias, who had been unable to speak since the appearance of the angel. Because Zacharias had not believed the word of the Lord at first, he had been struck dumb until the birth of the child as a sign of what God would do (see vv. 18-20). When the temple officials asked Zacharias what to name the child, he wrote: "His name is John" (v. 63). Once he had confirmed this, "his mouth was opened immediately, and his tongue loosed, and he spake, and praised God" (v. 64).

Why did God choose the name John for this special baby? It was a name that described what the

Lord would do for this couple—and for the world. The name comes from an Old Testament name, Johanan, a name meaning "Jehovah is gracious." It's a combination of the name Jehovah and a Hebrew word meaning "to be favorably inclined toward, to give graciously, to pity." In the Old Testament, we find ten men who were given the name Johanan. Likewise, five men of the New Testament had this name, including the Apostle John and John Mark.

In naming their child John, God was reminding Zacharias and Elisabeth of how gracious he had been in giving them this special son in their old age. But the name represented an even greater truth. John would be a living witness to the people of God's grace and mercy in sending His Son, the Messiah, to earth as their Saviour.

Every time we see or hear the name John, we should be reminded of the wonderful grace God has shown to us. We read in Psalm 86:15: "But thou, O Lord, art a God full of compassion, and gracious, longsuffering, and plenteous in mercy and truth." At times we may begin to wonder if God is gracious. We may doubt God's compassion when He doesn't answer our prayers when or how we think He should. When we are facing problems and pain, we tend to ask, "Has God forgotten to be gracious?" (77:9). The answer to that question is no. Our God and His Word never changes. The Lord is gracious and compassionate toward us at all times. Thus, even when we are burdened with problems, we can still believe that God is using these problems for our

111

good. We should never doubt His love or care for us.

What Is God's Grace?

In thinking of the graciousness of God, two questions come to mind. It is important that we know the answers to these questions in order to fully understand, and appreciate, the life we have in Christ. The first question we must ask is *"What is the grace of God?"* It is God's kindness toward undeserving sinners.

In the Bible we find a distinction made between grace and mercy. In showing us mercy, God does not give us what we deserve. On the other hand, the Lord shows us His grace by giving us what we don't deserve. All of this is made possible through the cross.

Of course, the grace of God does not mean that He overlooks our sin. The Lord is not a doting grandfather who closes his eyes and says, "Well, the children can't help themselves." We must remember that God's love and holiness never compete or conflict with each other. As a holy God, He must judge sin. As a loving God, He saves sinners. How can He do both? Through His grace.

What is grace? Grace is *God's riches at Christ's expense.* The Lord's holiness demanded a sacrifice for sins. So our loving God went to the cross and paid the price for our sins. Having paid the debt and upheld His holiness, God can now open the floodgates of His grace and pour it freely on us. The Apostle John wrote: "And of His fulness have all we received, and grace for [upon] grace" (John 1:16). Peter also talked a great deal about God's grace. He described the Lord as the "God of all grace" (I Pet. 5:10) and said that believers enjoy "the manifold grace of God" (4:10). God heaps one act of grace after another on us, even though we don't deserve it.

How can you know whether or not you are living by God's grace? If you see your life and everything in it as a gift from God, then you are living by grace. However, if you believe that you have earned—and therefore deserve—whatever honors and blessings come your way, then you really don't know much about God's grace. Everything we have—money, family, job, faith, eternal life—has been given to us by God, not because we deserve it but rather because He loves us so much. The longer we walk with the Lord, the more we discover how undeserving we really are.

Why Do We Need God's Grace?

This brings us to the second question about grace: *Why do we need God's grace?* The answer to this question is not as obvious as it might appear to be. In fact, the Scriptures list a number of reasons why it was necessary for God to show us grace. In these reasons we also find a pattern for living in grace.

Because We Are Sinners

The first, and most apparent, reason why we need God's grace is *because we are sinners.* Ephe-

113

sians 2:8,9 states, "For by grace are ye saved through faith; and that not of yourselves; it is the gift of God: not of works, lest any man should boast."

Many people today have the mistaken idea that as long as they are good, the Lord will take them to heaven. They say, "I've been an honest, moral person all my life. I take good care of my family. Why, I even go to church and give occasionally! I'm better than most people in the world." However, when they stand before God at the Judgment, their boasting will be in vain. They will realize that God does not save us because of our good works. Just one sin permanently stains our record so that God must judge us. Only His grace that comes through Jesus Christ can remove the guilt of our sins and make us righteous before Him.

Every person is born with a sinful nature. We are not sinners because we sin; rather, we sin because we are sinners. God has given man a choice, and we have chosen to disobey. Thus, we need God's grace because we are sinners.

Because We Are Servants

We need God's grace not only because we are sinners, but also *because we are His servants.* Once we accept Christ and receive the saving grace of God, we are given a job to do. Many days it becomes difficult to carry on our work. At these times, God gives us additional grace to complete the task He has called us to do.

God's grace is not a one-time gift. He continually gives us more grace to serve Him. The Apostle Paul had many physical afflictions, problems and burdens, yet he accomplished the impossible. How was he able to do it? Simply by relying on the grace of God. He stated, "For I am the least of the apostles, that am not meet [fit] to be called an apostle, because I persecuted the church of God. But by the grace of God I am what I am: and his grace which was bestowed upon me was not in vain; but I laboured more abundantly than they all: yet not I, but the grace of God which was with me" (I Cor. 15:9,10).

Being a servant of God is never easy. You must carry many heavy burdens and solve many tough problems. People will continually make life difficult for you. Like Paul, you realize that you cannot serve God in your strength; you must depend on His grace. When you give yourself to the God of all grace, He in turn gives you all the grace you need to serve Him. God doesn't call you and then leave you alone. He will equip you for the task, just as He equipped Moses, Paul and many others.

Because We Are Stewards

We also need God's grace *because we are stewards.* God has blessed us greatly. No matter how much or how little we may possess, whatever we have is from the hand of God, and He wants us to use it for His glory.

In II Corinthians 8:1,2 we find the secret for giving. We read: "Moreover, brethren, we do you to wit [testify] of the grace of God bestowed on the churches of Macedonia. How that in a great trial of

115

affliction the abundance of their joy and their deep poverty abounded unto the riches of their liberality." Even though the churches of Macedonia were living in deep poverty, by the grace of God, they gave liberally to meet the needs of others. What was their secret? They lived by this formula: Great trial plus deep poverty, mixed generously with God's grace and abundant joy, produces the riches of generosity.

We need God's grace in order to be the stewards He wants us to be. Giving is so hard for some people because they are living under the burden of law and works. In their eyes, giving is a duty or obligation. However, those who live by the grace of God realize that all of life is His gift. As such, giving becomes a joy and privilege. The grace of God within compels us to use what God has given us for His glory and for the good of others.

Because We Are Sufferers

A fourth reason why we need the grace of God is *because we are sufferers*. We live in a suffering world. Many believers today are going through intense physical or emotional suffering. Each day they live in pain and agony. Maybe doctors have done all they can for them. Perhaps they have prayed, but God has not seen fit to heal them. Does this mean that the Lord has abandoned them? Of course not. God never abandons us in our time of need. However, He frequently does use suffering to show us the depths of His grace and strength.

The Apostle Paul was plagued throughout his

116

ministry with some great affliction. Like us, he did not wish to suffer, so he asked the Lord three times to heal him. God did not choose to remove the affliction but instead showed Paul the purpose in it. In II Corinthians 12:7-9, Paul revealed the purpose of his suffering: "And lest I should be exalted above measure through the abundance of the revelations, there was given to me a thorn in the flesh, the messenger of Satan to buffet me, lest I should be exalted above measure. For this thing I besought the Lord thrice, that it might depart from me. And he said unto me, My grace is sufficient for thee: for my strength is made perfect in weakness."

Why would God permit Paul, who was doing such a great work for Him, to suffer so long? So he would not begin to be too proud (v. 7). Suffering has a way of humbling us and pointing us to God. Only when we are too weak to help ourselves does the reality of God's words sink in: "My grace is sufficient for thee: for my strength is made perfect in weakness" (v. 9).

Of course, God is able to heal us both physically and emotionally when this is His will. I have experienced God's healing in my life and have seen it in many others. I believe our God is big enough for every problem and burden we have. I also believe that God can be glorified when people are not healed. Sometimes the Lord sees fit to take away the affliction. At other times, He says, "You need this suffering. I'm going to let you keep it awhile longer."

Some of us may not understand until we get to

117

heaven why God permitted us to suffer, but we will all discover eventually that it was for our good. Meanwhile, the Lord will give us the grace we need for every trial. Even though God may not change our circumstances, He can—and will—change us. His grace and strength are sufficient, and they become most evident when we are the weakest.

Because We Are Soldiers

In writing to Timothy, Paul listed a fifth reason why we need the grace of God—*because we are God's soldiers*. In II Timothy 2:1,3 we read: "Thou therefore, my son, be strong in the grace that is in Christ Jesus. . . . Thou therefore endure hardness, as a good soldier of Jesus Christ."

The Christian life is not a playground; it's a battleground. Christians are constantly involved in a battle with Satan and his army of followers. The Apostle Peter warned us, "Be sober, be vigilant; because your adversary the devil, as a roaring lion, walketh about, seeking whom he may devour" (I Pet. 5:8). The world hates us and is constantly trying to destroy us. And our old sin nature would love to defeat us. The world, the flesh and the Devil all oppose us, and we must be good soldiers to survive.

How do we become a good soldier? By learning how to endure hardness, or hardship. We are living in a society that teaches us to enjoy softness. They tell us that our goal in life should be to obtain all the comforts we can. But as any soldier knows, the only way to properly prepare yourself for the rigors of

118

battle is by pushing yourself to the limit of your endurance as you train. And in our battle with Satan, our endurance is far too weak. We must rely on the strength of God's grace to win the battle.

Because We Are Students

But Christians are more than soldiers; they are also students. And *because we are students*, we need God's grace to understand the many important and complex truths found in His Word. Titus 2:11-13 tells us, "For the grace of God that bringeth salvation hath appeared to all men, teaching us that, denying ungodliness and worldly lusts, we should live soberly, righteously, and godly, in this present world; looking for that blessed hope, and the glorious appearing of the great God and our Saviour Jesus Christ."

In this passage we see that the grace of God not only brings us salvation but teaches us how to live as a Christian until the Lord returns. The school of life is the most difficult school in the world, and we are all enrolled in it. Without the grace of God to teach us, we would never pass the tests.

Have you ever considered just how wonderful it is to be one of God's students? Not only does our Teacher know everything, but He is kind, gentle and patient with us. The Great Teacher has told us, "Take my yoke upon you, and learn of me; for I am meek and lowly in heart: and ye shall find rest unto your souls" (Matt. 11:29).

As you read the Word of God, the Holy Spirit teaches you the truth of God. God's grace enables you to apply His Word in personal and practical ways to your daily situations and problems. God knows what you need today and has just the lesson for that need in His Word.

We need God's grace because we are sinners. If we are not saved by grace, we are not saved at all. We need God's grace because we are servants. If our work is not motivated and energized by the grace of God, it won't last. We need grace because we are God's stewards. His grace enables us to make good use of all that He has given us. We need God's grace because we are sufferers who need to have victory in, and over, pain and circumstances. We need God's grace because we are soldiers engaged in a fierce battle. And we need God's grace because we are students who still have much to learn in His school of life.

Are you living by the grace of God? Are you saying with Paul, "By the grace of God I am what I am" (I Cor. 15:10)? When we finally see life as a gift, we will stop striving to deserve—and begin believing and receiving—God's abundant grace. John the Baptist was born through the graciousness of God, and you can receive this grace as well. So "come boldly unto the throne of grace, that [you] may obtain mercy, and find grace to help in time of need" (Heb. 4:16).

Chapter 11

The Greatest Baby of All

Jesus Christ

The Bible contains two well-known names that we would not choose for our sons. We would avoid the one name because it is too shameful and the other because it is too wonderful. The shameful name is Judas. While the meaning of the name is good, the man associated with the name stands for dishonesty and deceit. The name itself comes from the name Judah, which means "praise." Judas, the betrayer, took this honorable name and ruined it.

Likewise, we would avoid choosing the second name because of the man associated with it. However, the reason for not choosing this name is vastly different. It is too wonderful and holy to be associated with any human being. That name, of course, is Jesus Christ. The name Jesus means "saviour." It was a familiar name in Bible times. In fact, the works of the Jewish historian Josephus lists 20 different men who had this name. But the name dropped out of common usage about the second century. Since then, most people in English-speaking countries have avoided naming their sons Jesus.

While you may not be named Jesus, it is still one of the most commonly used names in the world. We can't avoid the name of Jesus Christ. We find it in art, literature and music. It is exalted in the work of the Church. While many great names in history—Napoleon Bonaparte, Winston Churchill, George Washington—are remembered and respected today, we are not required to respond in any way to these names. We can ignore them if we choose. However, the name of Jesus demands some response. When we hear this name, we must do something with it. We must either accept or reject the Person who wears the name "Saviour." We can use this name to swear against man, or we can use it to exalt the Almighty God.

Understand the Name

How should we respond to the name of the Lord Jesus? I would like to suggest five responses that God desires from us as we consider the name of Jesus. First, He wants us to *understand the name*.

While knowing the meanings of our names is intriguing, it really isn't important. I have a collection of books in my library that explain the meanings of different names. It's interesting to note how even the well-known scholars don't always agree on the meaning, derivation or background of a name—even a common name. But the definition of a name does not matter; it's the person who gives meaning to the name. When I was engaged, I didn't ask my fiancée what her name meant. Her name made no difference. I was only concerned with the person.

The name Jesus comes from the name Joshua, which means "Jehovah is salvation." Numbers 13:8 records the origin of this name: "Of the tribe of Ephraim, Oshea the son of Nun." Joshua, who succeeded Moses as the leader of the Israelites, was originally named Oshea, a name meaning "salvation" or "deliverance." Moses took his name and added the word Jehovah to it. In the same passage, we later read: "And Moses called Oshea the son of Nun Jehoshua" (v. 16). Moses renamed Joshua to remind the Children of Israel of what the Lord had done, and would do, in delivering them. Likewise, God gave His Son a name that would be a testimony to every person of the salvation He has given us.

In Bible times it was the custom for the father to choose the names for his children. Notice that Joseph did not choose the name for Jesus. Why? He was not the father. The Lord Jesus was conceived by the Holy Spirit and born of the virgin Mary. Thus God, His Father, chose the name.

As you study the Bible, you will discover that God chose the names for several important babies rather than leaving that task to their fathers. The phrase "thou shalt call his name" appears four times in the Scriptures. It's interesting to note the names the Lord chose in each case. When Hagar fled after she became pregnant with Abraham's child, the angel of the Lord appeared to her in the desert and said, "Behold, thou art with child, and shalt bear a son, and shalt call his name Ishmael; because the Lord hath heard thy affliction" (Gen. 16:11). The name Ishmael means "God will hear." The Lord

123

chose this name for Hagar's son to remind her of how He had heard and helped her in her distress.

God also chose the name for Abraham's second son, the son of promise. In Genesis 17:19 we read: "And God said, Sarah thy wife shall bear thee a son indeed; and thou shalt call his name Isaac: and I will establish my covenant with him for an everlasting covenant, and with his seed after him." The name Isaac means "laughter" and was a reminder to Abraham and Sarah of how they had laughed at the promise of God—Abraham in joy and Sarah in unbelief.

The first two names chosen by God for children in the Bible were names that typify spiritual truths. Ishmael represents the flesh. He was born because of Abraham's impatience and unbelief. Isaac, who represents the Spirit, was born because of Abraham's and Sarah's faith in God. While Isaac brought joy, Ishmael brought trial.

The third baby named by God in the Bible was John the Baptist. Luke 1:13 records, "But the angel said unto him, Fear not, Zacharias: for thy prayer is heard; and thy wife Elisabeth shall bear thee a son, and thou shalt call his name John." The name John means "God is gracious." This baby was sent by God to prepare the way for the Messiah who would bring God's grace to the world.

Shortly after the angel's appearance to Zacharias, we find the wonderful announcement to Mary: "And, behold, thou shalt conceive in thy womb, and bring forth a son, and shalt call his name Jesus [Jehoshua, "Jehovah is salvation"]" (v. 31). God again confirmed His choice of the name for His Son when the angel appeared to Joseph and told him, "Joseph, thou son of David, fear not to take unto thee Mary thy wife: for that which is conceived in her is of the Holy Ghost. And she shall bring forth a son, and thou shalt call his name Jesus: for he shall save his people from their sins" (Matt. 1:20,21). According to the Lord's instructions, when the time came to circumcise the baby, Mary and Joseph gave him the name Jesus (see Luke 2:21).

It's interesting to note that there are no recorded births in Scripture after the birth of the Lord Jesus Christ. Likewise, the last genealogy listed in the New Testament is that of Jesus. From this we can see how all previously recorded biblical history pointed the way to the birth of this baby and to this name. Once Jesus came, any other records were no longer needed. Thus, God is saying to us, in effect, "The only birth I'm concerned about is the new birth, the second birth. That's why My Son came."

Because a number of men who lived during the time of Christ were also named Jesus (Jehoshua), other names were used in conjunction with His name. He was frequently associated with his hometown and parents. In telling Nathanael about Jesus, Philip said, "We have found him, of whom Moses in the law, and the prophets, did write, Jesus of Nazareth, the son of Joseph. And Nathanael said unto him, Can there any good thing come out of Nazareth?" (John 1:45,46). Jesus' association with Nazareth underscored the fact that He was "despised

125

and rejected of men" (Isa. 53:3). He was also called Jesus the Christ. The Greek word translated "Christ" means "anointed one." It is the equivalent of the Hebrew word "Messiah." This name emphasized that Jesus was the promised Messiah sent by God to redeem the world.

Trust the Name

Understanding the name of Jesus is important in realizing what He has done for us. But our second response to His name is even more crucial. Once we understand it, we should *trust the name.*

What is the difference between the name of Jesus and the names of other influencial people in history? The difference is that we cannot trust the names of Thomas Edison, Albert Einstein or anyone else to help us. But we can trust the name of the Lord Jesus because He is still alive and at work in the world today. True to His name, Jesus is our salvation: "Thou shalt call his name Jesus: for he shall save his people from their sins" (Matt. 1:21).

What does this salvation mean to us? It means we have been delivered from condemnation. We are set free from spiritual bondage and given a new purpose in life. This salvation brings healing and soundness to the inner person and victory over failure. It assures us of protection and safety so we need not fear. Salvation through the name of Jesus gives us new power.

The name of Jesus is powerful. In the Book of Acts, you find the apostles performing great miracles in the name of Jesus. You find them pray-

126

ing in the name of Jesus. Peter's healing of a lame man in Acts 3 is a prime example. When Peter saw the man begging at the temple gate, he told him, "In the name of Jesus Christ of Nazareth rise up and walk" (v. 6). Peter lifted the man to his feet, and he was immediately healed. The man began to jump and leap and praise the Lord (see vv. 7,8). Peter's own power did not heal the lame man; it was the power of the name of Jesus.

But in order to enjoy this salvation and power, we must make the name of Jesus personal. We must trust the name of Jesus Christ. This involves more than a mere surface belief in the meaning of His name. It demands a complete dedication of our lives to the *Person* of Jesus. For instance, no doubt you have heard people say, "Stay away from him. He has a bad name." What do they mean? Is it that this person's parents made a mistake in naming him? No, they are saying that his character cannot be trusted. Thus, when we trust in the name of Jesus, we are placing our faith in His holy and blameless character. Jesus Christ has a name we can trust.

Making the name of Jesus personal also involves making Him our Saviour. Many non-Christians in the world today acknowledge the fact that Jesus is *a* saviour. However, they believe that He is just one of many. This is not trust. We must believe that Jesus is *the* Saviour. The Apostle John wrote: "The Father sent the Son to be the Saviour of the world" (I John 4:14). But we can't stop there either. We must make Him *my* Saviour. Mary said, "My soul doth magnify the Lord, and my spirit hath rejoiced in God my Saviour" (Luke 1:46,47). It's not enough to say that He is a saviour or the Saviour. In order to really trust the name of Jesus, we must make Him the Lord and Saviour of our entire life. Have you made the name of Jesus personal?

Honor the Name

The third response we need to make to the name of Jesus is to *honor the name*. God has honored the name of Jesus above every name, and He expects us to do the same. We read in Philippians 2:9-11: "Wherefore God also hath highly exalted him, and given him a name which is above every name: that at the name of Jesus every knee should bow, of things in heaven, and things in earth, and things under the earth; and that every tongue should confess that Jesus Christ is Lord, to the glory of God the Father."

When we accept Christ as our Saviour, we are united with Him and are given His name. We wear the name "Christian" for everyone to see. People know by our name that we have been saved and belong to Christ. Thus, anything we do or say reflects on the good name of Jesus. Are your words and works bringing honor or disgrace to the name of Jesus? Can people look at your life and glorify God? "Let your light so shine before men, that they may see your good works and glorify your Father which is in heaven" (Matt. 5:16).

One day every person will bow before Jesus Christ and confess that He is Lord. For some, this will mean condemnation, because they rejected the name of Jesus on earth. For others—those who honored and accepted the Lord—it will mean eternal glorification and blessings. It is not important for people to honor our names. What matters is that Christ's name is honored. Start today to honor the name of Jesus.

Rejoice in the Name

Once we understand the name of Jesus and all it means to us, trust in His name and honor His name, we will find that we can also *rejoice in the name.* Praising and rejoicing in the name of Jesus should flow naturally from the hearts of those who have experienced His salvation.

Time and time again in the New Testament we find that when people encountered the name of Jesus, their first reaction was to praise Him. When Zacharias learned that his promised son would prepare the way for the coming Messiah, Jesus Christ, he burst forth in praise, saying, "Blessed be the Lord God of Israel; for he hath visited and redeemed his people, and hath raised up an horn of salvation for us in the house of his servant David; . . . that we should be saved from our enemies" (Luke 1:68, 69,71). In verse 77 he added, "To give knowledge of salvation unto his people by the remission of their sins." What was this old priest talking about? Salvation in Jesus.

The virgin Mary also praised Him for this salvation (see v. 47). The angels announced it at His birth: "For unto you is born this day in the city of David a Saviour, which is Christ the Lord" (2:11).

When Simeon, who had waited his entire life for the promise, saw the baby Jesus at the temple, he exclaimed, "Lord, now lettest thou thy servant depart in peace, according to thy word: for mine eyes have seen thy salvation" (vv. 29,30). These people rejoiced in the name of Jesus. Are you truly rejoicing and praising God for the salvation you have received in Christ?

Proclaim the Name

It is not enough just to claim the name of Jesus and His salvation for ourselves. We must also *proclaim the name.* We live in a world that needs to know the saving power of Jesus. The name of Jesus is the only name that can conquer sin, death and Satan. It is the only name that gives us power in prayer.

When I read the Gospels and the Book of Acts, I see the power of the name of Jesus displayed as believers proclaimed His name. Peter stated emphatically, "For there is none other name under heaven given among men, whereby we must be saved" (Acts 4:12). When the apostles were brought before the temple leaders and commanded to stop witnessing and performing miracles in the name of Jesus (v. 18), they boldly replied, "We cannot but speak the things which we have seen and heard" (v. 20). These men were compelled to proclaim the name of Jesus.

We must be careful not to begin proclaiming our names or the names of our ministries or churches. Jesus Christ is our *only* message and our sole purpose for being on earth. The Lord has called us to be His witnesses (see Matt. 28:18-20). Millions of people in the world today have never heard the name of Jesus. Our task as Christians is to become so excited by the power and glory of His name that we are compelled to share that name with others.

Do you understand the name of Jesus? Are you trusting the name of Jesus and making Him *your* Saviour? Are you honoring His name and rejoicing in His name? Are you proclaiming His name? "Thou shalt call his name Jesus: for he shall save his people from their sins" (1:21).

Chapter 12

Your New Name

Some children reach a point in their lives when they dislike their name and want to change it. Sometimes their friends do it for them, pinning a nickname on them that they don't want and can't get rid of. Once they reach adulthood, some will even go to court and legally change their name.

People change their names for various other reasons as well. They do this in a number of ways. The most common name change for women takes place if they marry and assume their husband's surname. In countries where there is a monarchy, the king or queen will sometimes bestow a title, such as the Duke of Bedford or the Duke of Leicester, on a faithful subject. Or you can change your name yourself, asking your friends and acquaintances to call you by this new name. Writers often assume a new name, writing under pen names. Actors, actresses, musicians and other various entertainers also frequently change their names. I have a book in my library that lists the real names of famous people. After reading the book, I can understand why many of them changed their names!

The Word of God also describes another way to

receive a new name—by experiencing the new birth in Christ. When we accept Christ as our Saviour, we are given His name—Christian. What does this new name mean for us? In the Bible, receiving a new name means much more than just adding a new title, label or identification, for the name reveals the character of the person. Every name for God in the Scriptures describes an important aspect of His character. Thus, when God gives us a new name, we become a new person. We have a new beginning, a new life and a new character.

In Revelation 2:17 we read: "To him that overcometh will I give to eat of the hidden manna, and will give him a white stone, and in the stone a new name written, which no man knoweth saving he that receiveth it." The word translated "new" in this passage is referring to quality rather than to time, or age. We are given a new kind of name, a new kind of life. Paul was referring to this new quality of life when he wrote: "Like as Christ was raised up from the dead by the glory of the Father, even so we also should walk in newness of life" (Rom. 6:4). When we accept Christ, we are transformed into a new person with an entirely different kind of life. "Therefore if any man be in Christ, he is a new creature [creation]: old things are passed away; behold, all things are become new" (II Cor. 5:17).

Thus, the only way to receive this new name from God is to become a new person. And the only way to become a new person is by experiencing a new birth. We read about this new birth in John 3:1-3: "There was a man of the Pharisees, named

133

Nicodemus, a ruler of the Jews: the same came to Jesus by night, and said unto him, Rabbi, we know that thou art a teacher come from God: for no man can do these miracles that thou doest, except God be with him. Jesus answered and said unto him, Verily, verily, I say unto thee, Except a man be born again, he cannot see the kingdom of God." Notice that in the four verses that follow this passage the word "born" is used six times: "Nicodemus saith unto him, How can a man be born when he is old? can he enter the second time into his mother's womb, and be born? Jesus answered, Verily, verily, I say unto thee, Except a man be born of water [human birth] and of the Spirit [divine birth], he cannot enter into the kingdom of God. That which is born of the flesh is flesh; and that which is born of the Spirit is spirit. Marvel not that I said unto thee, Ye must be born again" (vv. 4-7).

In this passage, the Lord described salvation as a birth process. Why would the Lord Jesus use birth as a picture of salvation? I think He did it because of the comparisons we can see between them. It's important that we understand these comparisons because, as we have seen from the lives of many in the Old Testament, God has rejected our first birth. He will accept only our second birth—the time when we are born again, or born from above, by trusting Christ.

Birth Is a Universal Experience

While many comparisons can be drawn between physical birth and spiritual birth, I'd like to focus on

134

eight that have special significance. First, we see that *birth is a universal experience.*

The Bible gives us many pictures of salvation. Our Lord pictured salvation as a shepherd finding a lost sheep (see Luke 15:3-7). However, since most of us have never been shepherds and some have never even seen a sheep, this may be hard to relate to. Likewise, salvation is compared to a prodigal son who comes home after wasting his father's money (see vv. 11-24). Few of us have probably experienced this either. Salvation is also compared to the resurrection of the dead (see John 5:21; 11:23-26). Very few people today would claim to have seen anyone raised from the dead. But birth is one picture of salvation that everyone understands. We can all identify with birth, because it is a universal experience. This fact also indicates to us that every person needs to experience this new spiritual birth.

Birth Involves Life

The second comparison is that *birth involves life.* This world contains several levels, or kingdoms, of life. First, we have a mineral kingdom where there is no life at all. Then we have a plant kingdom, an animal kingdom, a human kingdom and a divine kingdom. God has ordained that no kingdom can lift itself up to a higher level. Stones can't become vegetables, vegetables can't become animals, animals can't transform themselves into humans, and no human being can lift himself up into God's kingdom. However, God has ordained that each king-

135

dom can reach down and pull the kingdom below it up. So we find that plants reach down into the mineral kingdom and turn minerals into plants. An animal comes along and eats the plant, which causes the plant to become part of the animal. The human being, in turn, eats the animal, and the animal becomes part of the human.

In a similar way, God reached down into this world to lift humans up to His kingdom. John 3:13 says, "And no man hath ascended up to heaven, but he that came down from heaven, even the Son of man which is in heaven." Christ came down from heaven in order to lift us up. And for the believer it starts with the new birth, for birth involves life.

What is required for life? We must have four basic necessities—light, air, water and food. We can see these same four requirements in our spiritual life. And Jesus Christ is all of these. He is the light of the world. John 1:4 says, "In him was life; and the life was the light of men." The Holy Spirit is compared to air: "The wind bloweth where it listeth [wills], and thou hearest the sound thereof, but canst not tell whence it cometh, and whither it goeth: so is every one that is born of the Spirit" (3:8). Jesus also described Himself as the water of life (4:14) and the bread of life (6:35). Spiritual birth involves life—a life that is eternal and abundant.

Birth Requires Two Parents

In comparing physical birth with spiritual birth, we also see that *birth requires two parents.* Every human being who enters this world has both a biological father and mother. Likewise, two parents are involved in our spiritual birth. One parent is the Spirit of God. Jesus told us, "Except a man be born . . . of the Spirit, he cannot enter into the kingdom of God" (John 3:15). The second spiritual parent is the Word of God. In I Peter 1:23 we read: "Being born again, not of corruptible seed, but of incorruptible, by the word of God, which liveth and abideth for ever." What is this "word of God"? Peter told us in verse 25: "And this is the word which by the gospel is preached unto you."

When Jesus told Nicodemus that he must be born again, Nicodemus did not understand this concept of spiritual parentage. He was thinking only in physical terms. He asked Jesus, "How can a man . . . enter the second time into his mother's womb, and be born?" (John 3:4). Jesus replied, "Except a man be born of water [physical birth] and of the Spirit, he cannot enter into the kingdom of God. That which is born of the flesh is flesh; and that which is born of the Spirit is spirit" (vv. 5,6). How is a person born into God's family? The Spirit of God takes the Word of God and through it implants the life of God in you when you trust Jesus Christ as your Saviour.

Birth Determines Nature

The fourth comparison is that *birth determines our nature*. In the physical realm, every living creature inherits the nature of its breed at birth. For

137

example, a kitten always has the nature of a cat. A kitten will never inherit the nature of a dog. In the same way, when you are born again into God's family, you receive God's nature. We read in II Peter 1:4: "Whereby are given unto us exceeding great and precious promises: that by these ye might be partakers of the divine nature."

Being a child of God involves more than belonging to a church or talking like a Christian. It means that we have God's nature in us. When you are born of God, the Spirit of God uses the Word of God to impart the very nature of God within you. You are born again and become a new person through Jesus Christ. Your new name comes from your new nature.

Our birth determines our nature, and our nature determines how we will live. For example, our appetite and eating habits are determined by our nature. For 16 years my family owned a cat who was very fastidious about what it ate. Yet there are other animals that really don't care what they eat. Likewise, each animal's eating habits are different. You will not find a pig eating the way a sheep does or vice versa. Birth determines our appetite because birth determines our nature. Thus, when we are born into God's family, we have a spiritual hunger.

Nature also determines your environment. Eagles soar into the heavens, while fish swim in the waters. If you put the eagle underwater and the fish in the air, it would kill them. They cannot live out of their environment. The Christian's environment is Jesus

138

Christ. We have His nature; therefore, we must continually live in Him. If we wander away from Him, we begin to die spiritually.

In addition, our nature determines our associations. Fish swim together in schools with other fish. Likewise, you seldom find a sheep alone in a herd of cattle. Animals, by instinct, associate and breed with their own kind. In the same way, Christians like to be with other Christians. We are bonded together because we have the same nature, the same birth and the same Heavenly Father.

Our birth determines our nature, and our nature will determine our destiny. Where we will spend eternity depends on the kind of nature we have. If a person has a sinful nature and never receives the new nature, he wouldn't be happy in heaven, even if he could go there. Our destiny is shaped by our nature.

Birth Is Accompanied by Travail

In looking at birth, we discover another important truth: *Both physical and spiritual birth are accompanied by travail.* Even with all of our modern scientific equipment, a mother descends into the valley of death each time she gives birth to a child. In the same way, Jesus Christ our Lord travailed on the cross. Isaiah 53:11 tells us, "He shall see of the travail of his soul, and shall be satisfied." In order for us to be born into God's family, Jesus had to suffer agony on the cross. He had to die so we could live. He had to walk through the darkness

139

so that we might be born into God's everlasting kingdom of light. Birth involves travail.

Birth Means Coming From Darkness to Light

In addition, we see that *birth involves coming out of darkness into light.* A baby spends the first nine months of his life in the darkness of his mother's womb. The first thing a baby sees after he leaves the womb is a world of light. The same is true of our spiritual birth.

Throughout the Scriptures, we find the contrast between the world and Christ described as darkness and light. Jesus told Nicodemus, "He that believeth on him [Christ] is not condemned: but he that believeth not is condemned already, because he hath not believed in the name of the only begotten Son of God. And this is the condemnation, that light is [has] come into the world, and men loved darkness rather than light, because their deeds were evil. For every one that doeth evil hateth the light, neither cometh to the light, lest his deeds should be reproved. But he that doeth truth cometh to the light, that his deeds may be made manifest, that they are wrought in God" (John 3:18-21).

It's interesting to note that when Nicodemus first came to Jesus, he came at night (see v. 2). However, the next time we read about Nicodemus, we find him in broad daylight, taking Jesus down from the cross and preparing Him for burial (see 19:38-42). He was no longer afraid to identify himself with the Lamb of God. He had been born into the family of God. When we accept Christ as our Saviour, we move from the spiritual darkness of sin into His marvelous light (see I Pet. 2:9).

Birth Involves the Future

The seventh truth we see as we compare physical and spiritual birth is that *birth involves the future.* There are two places you will rarely find a policeman waiting to arrest someone—a cemetery and the maternity ward of a hospital. While the police could arrest someone visiting a cemetery or hospital, you will never find them taking a corpse or a newborn baby into custody. Why? The dead have no future on earth, and a newborn has no past to convict him.

When a baby comes into the world, he has only a future ahead of him. Likewise, when you are born again into the family of God, your past is forgotten. Your slate of sins is wiped clean by God's forgiveness. You have a new future before you and can look forward to a wonderful life with Him on earth and an eternity with Him in heaven. No wonder Peter wrote: "God . . . hath begotten us again [caused us to be born again] unto a lively [living] hope by the resurrection of Jesus Christ from the dead" (I Pet. 1:3). Our spiritual birth gives us a hope and a future. No one can even imagine the blessings awaiting us in heaven. "Eye hath not seen, nor ear heard, neither have entered into the heart of man, the things which God hath prepared for them that love him" (I Cor. 2:9).

In my pastoral ministry I've had the privilege of performing the wedding ceremony for many

141

couples. I've also had the joy of seeing new life come into their homes and of dedicating these babies to the Lord. When a couple discovers they are going to have a baby, they make many preparations in anticipation of the new arrival—a special room, new furniture and new clothing. They can hardly wait for their child to come. In the same way, our Saviour in heaven is preparing a place for us (John 14:2,3). We have been born again unto a living hope. We have a hope and a future that grows bigger and brighter every day.

Birth Is Final

Finally, in comparing physical and spiritual birth, we see that *birth is final.* You cannot be unborn. Even if a baby dies, he is still a person with a soul and a spirit. He has still been born into a family. Each birth takes place at a point in time, once and for all. And in a normal birth, the baby is born with everything he needs. You never find parents returning a month later to pick up their baby's ears or feet. The baby is complete. All he needs to do from then on is grow and develop.

Our spiritual birth is also a one-time act. When you are born into God's family, you are born complete in Christ (Col. 2:10). Then, like a baby, you begin the growth process. The requirements for growth are the same: food (the Word of God), exercise (the service of God), love (fellowship with God and with His people), cleansing (confession and righteous living). When these elements are present, we will grow into the image of our Father.

142

When a baby is born, that birth is final. His genetic structure has already been determined at conception. The same is true of our spiritual birth. When we are born into God's family, the Lord equips us spiritually to serve Him. In God's family, members need not compete with each other for attention or rewards. There is no room for envy or strife. We don't need to be envious of other people's gifts or abilities, for whatever gifts we possess have been given to us by God. He will reward us, not according to our gifts but according to our faithfulness.

The Lord has pictured salvation as birth, because it is a universal experience we can all understand. Like our physical birth, spiritual birth produces an entirely new life in us. We have two parents—the Spirit of God and the Word of God—imparting this new life to us. This spiritual birth determines how we will live and act. It gives us a hope and a future as we come out of the darkness of sin and live in the light of our Lord. Spiritual birth takes place once; it is final. The cost of our new birth was very expensive. Jesus had to suffer intense agony and death on the cross in order that we might live.

New birth is not a luxury; it is a necessity. God will not accept our first birth. Jesus has plainly told us, "You must be born again." When we experience this new birth through faith in Jesus Christ, we become part of the greatest family on earth—God's family. And we are given the best name of all—the name Christian.

Some Bible Names and Their Meanings

Bible scholars disagree on the meaning of some names.
These are the generally accepted meanings.

Girls

Bernice — victorious
Claudia — lame
Deborah — bee (contains the idea of orderly
or systematic motion)
Dorcas — gazelle
Drusilla — watered by the dew
Elisabeth — God is my oath
Esther — star
Eunice — conquering well, victorious
Eve — life-giver
Hannah — grace, favor
Joanna — gift of God
Julia — soft-haired; youthful
Lois — agreeable
Lydia — from Lydia (region in Asia); travailing
Martha — lady, mistress of the home
Mary — Greek equivalent of the Hebrew name Miriam
Miriam — obstinacy, rebellion, bitterness
Naomi — my pleasantness, delight
Phebe — radiant, shining
Priscilla — little; ancient
Rachel — ewe
Rebekah — rope, noose (in a flattering sense, contains the
idea of a maiden who ensnares by her beauty)
Rhoda — rose
Ruth — friend, companion
Sarah — princess
Susanna — lily

Boys

Aaron — enlightened, illumined
Adam — earth, possibly red earth
Andrew — manly
Barnabas — son of encouragement
Benjamin — son of my right hand
Cornelius — of a horn
Daniel — God is my judge
David — beloved; possibly chieftain
Jacob — one who takes by the heel, supplanter
James — Greek equivalent of the Hebrew name Jacob
Jason — healing
Joel — Jehovah is God
John — Jehovah is gracious
Jonathan — Jehovah has given, Jehovah's gift
Joseph — adding, may Jehovah add
Joshua — Jehovah is salvation
Luke — from Lucania (district in southern Italy);
　　　light-giving
Mark — defense
Matthew — gift of the Lord
Nicolas — conqueror of the people, victory of the people
Paul — little
Peter — stone, rock
Philip — lover of horses
Reuben — behold a son
Rufus — red, red-haired
Samuel — asked of God
Silas — woody
Simon — hearing
Stephen — crown
Thomas — twin
Timothy — honoring God
Zacharias — Jehovah is renowned

Top 10 Names in the United States
(Based on 1983 statistics)

Girls	Boys
1. Jennifer	1. Michael
2. Sarah, Sara	2. Christopher
3. Jessica	3. Matthew
4. Nicole, Nichole	4. James
5. Amanda	5. Brian, Bryan
6. Ashley	6. Jason
7. Megan, Meghan	7. Andrew
8. Elizabeth	8. Adam
9. Katherine, Kathryn, Catherine	9. Joshua
10. Lindsay, Lindsey	10. David

Our Choices

Boy	**Girl**
1. _____	1. _____
2. _____	2. _____
3. _____	3. _____
4. _____	4. _____

(Round TWO)

1. _____	1. _____
2. _____	2. _____
3. _____	3. _____
4. _____	4. _____

Back to the Bible is a nonprofit ministry dedicated to Bible teaching, evangelism and edification of Christians worldwide.

If we may assist you in knowing more about Christ and the Christian life, please write to us without obligation:

Back to the Bible
P.O. Box 82808
Lincoln, NE 68501